A GUIDE TO THE

BUILDINGS
of
COVENTRY

GEORGE DEMIDOWICZ

A GUIDE TO THE

BUILDINGS
of
COVENTRY

AN ILLUSTRATED
ARCHITECTURAL HISTORY

TEMPUS

Frontispiece: Ford's Hospital, interior courtyard.

First published 2003

Tempus Publishing Limited
The Mill, Brimscombe Port,
Stroud, Gloucestershire, GL5 2QG
www.tempus-publishing.com

British Library Cataloguing in Publication Data.
A catalogue record for this book is available from the British Library.

ISBN 0 7524 3115 3

Typesetting and origination by Tempus Publishing Limited
Printed in Great Britain by Midway Colour Print, Wiltshire

CONTENTS

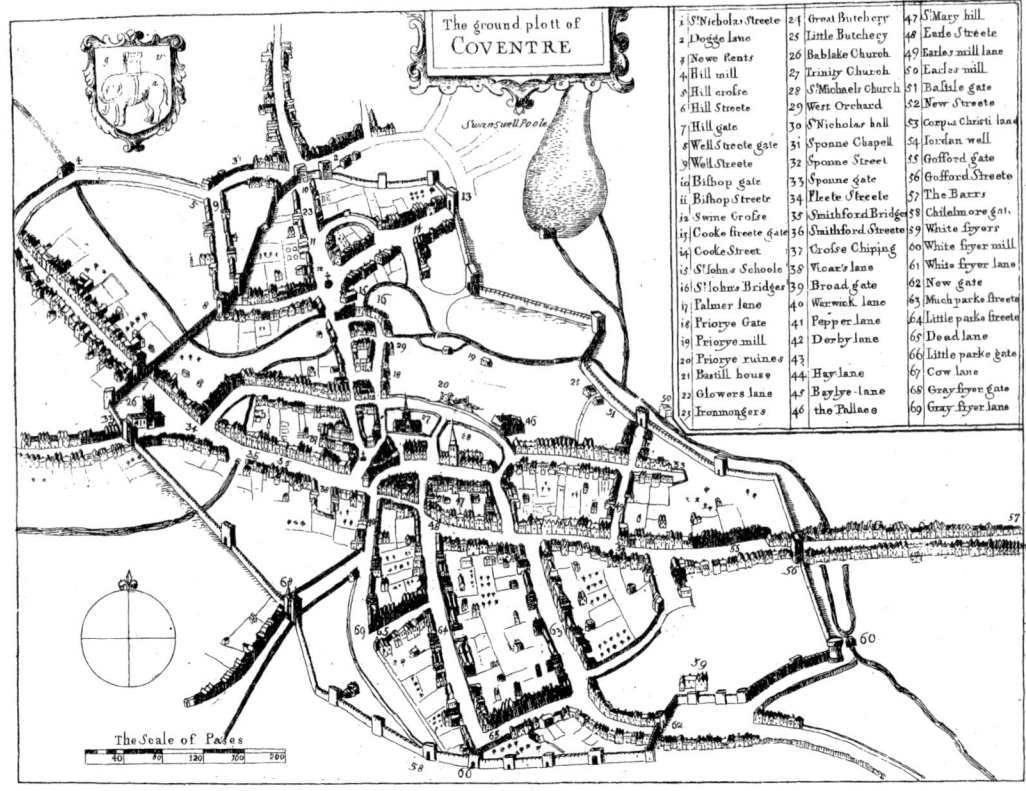

John Speed's map of Coventry, *c.* 1610.

FOREWORD AND ACKNOWLEDGEMENTS

The Millennium was a double celebration for Coventry because the city itself could boast a thousand years of history. This was a theme taken up by Coventry's own Millennium Scheme: the Phoenix Initiative. A series of squares has been created, marching down the hill from the historic heart of the city to the Museum of British Road Transport, an unashamed symbol of twentieth-century Coventry and probably of times yet to come.

The buildings featured in this book span nine hundred years, if not the whole millennium. A fragment of stonework uncovered in the Phoenix excavations in St Mary's Cathedral may in fact belong to the abbey church founded by Leofric and Godiva, sometime in the 1020s or 1030s. With nearly a thousand statutorily and locally listed buildings in the city, it has been extremely difficult to select only about one hundred and twenty for illustration. Only a handful more have found their way into the text. For many of the buildings selected there were several other contenders.

Buildings capture national and local changes in architectural styles and construction techniques that have been used over many centuries. Losses and gains to the building stock reflect Coventry's past economic health. Buildings, like historical documents, can also be precious in their own right and the best and most interesting are now preserved for future generations to use and appreciate. It is a shame that, even when we have visually impressive buildings, they cannot be left to speak for themselves and suffer increasingly from misguided attempts to 'brighten things up'.

Although I write as a private individual and the views expressed are my own, this book has obviously been influenced by the twelve years I have spent as the City's Conservation Officer. I have been ably assisted in this task by Mark Singlehurst and I am very grateful to him for reading the drafts of this book and making many useful suggestions. My wife, Toni Demidowicz, and colleagues, Iain Soden and Kevin Wilkins, have also been extremely helpful with their comments. Last but not least, the work of Zenon Demidowicz, who took most of the photographs, is very gratefully acknowledged and this book has gained much from his labours in seeking the 'right shot.'

A nineteenth-century engraving of Great Butcher Row, which was demolished in 1936-37 to make way for Trinity Street.

HISTORICAL
BACKGROUND
1

The first recorded event in Coventry's history is the founding of a monastery consecrated in 1043 by Leofric, the Anglo-Saxon Earl of Mercia, and his countess, Godiva. Before this, all that is certain is the derivation of the city's name, which appears to have come into existence in the seventh or eighth century. It means Cofa's tree (*Cofan–treo(w)*) but it is not known who Cofa was, where the tree was situated and why it was special enough to be given a name. There is no evidence that the name Coventry was derived from *convent*, after the nunnery supposedly founded by an abbess, Osburga, in the early tenth century and destroyed by the Danes in 1016.

It has recently been suggested that in the Anglo-Saxon period Coventry was the centre of a large estate, and, since large estates very often contained a minster church, Coventry must therefore have had such an establishment. The argument for the existence of a church before Leofric and Godiva's foundation is complicated and much of it is highly speculative, reflecting the desperate lack of information we have on Coventry before the middle of the eleventh century.

The entry for Coventry in the Domesday Book in 1086 records an agricultural population of over sixty households. These were not necessarily concentrated in one place. Coventry was undoubtedly the centre of a large estate or manor that stretched from Allesley in the west to Wyken in the east and from Exhall in the north to Stivichall in the south. It also included Foleshill, Keresley and Stoke. Each of these places could have claimed a few tenants. Coventry may only have been the largest of a scatter of hamlets and individual farmsteads across this extensive manor. The possibility that it was already a town at this time and that this fact was omitted from the survey is an additional complication.

Although it is no longer believed that the Coventry district was once impenetrable forest, only gradually cleared by Anglo-Saxon settlers, the population density recorded by Domesday was low even by Warwickshire standards; heavy clays that were difficult to plough have been given as the cause. The more open and closely settled areas lay to the south and east along the lighter, gravelly soils of the Sowe and Avon valleys. It was in this kind of territory that the Roman fort at the Lunt in Baginton, on the south-east side of modern Coventry, was established in the first century AD.

Sometime in the late eleventh century, the Earl of Chester acquired the Coventry estate from the Crown with the result that it looked to the north and west for much of the early medieval period. In about 1100 the Bishop of Chester, Robert de Limesey, transferred his see south to Coventry. It has been suggested that this was an unlikely move, unless Coventry was already a town. Urban settlement would explain Leofric and Godiva's choice of location for their monastic foundation and why the bishop later followed them, converting their monastery church into his cathedral and their abbey into a priory. There is no doubt that the priory stimulated the growth of Coventry. A great market place was laid out in front of the west end of the church, which would extend today from the High Street to Ironmonger Row, taking in Broadgate and the whole of the site of the present Alders department store. Bishop Street, heading directly north from the market area, was part of this original plan. The Earls of Chester must also have played a part in the town's expansion, for, by the end of the eleventh century, they had established a castle to the south of the priory and developed their own market area. The axis of the Earl's development ran east-west along the route from Gosford to Spon with a relatively small market area at the extremities of High Street and Smithford Street connected to the Prior's Market to the north. It appears that the prior had taken the initiative in town growth with the earl following suit. The destruction of the castle following the civil wars of the mid-twelfth century allowed room for an extension of urban development in this prime location. The position of the earlier agricultural settlement of Coventry in the growing medieval town is unknown.

The division of Coventry into the Prior's Half and Earl's Half has dominated much historical writing on the medieval town but is no longer thought to have been as clear or to have lasted so long as earlier believed. By 1250 the successor to the Earls of Chester, Roger Montalt, had leased his inheritance to the priory for the yearly sum of £100 and the prior was lord of both halves. The unity of the lordships was to last about a hundred years and, during this period, Coventry's growth and reputation as a manufacturing and trading centre began to focus on the townsfolk acting independently of their lord. About 1330 the Montalt line died out and the Dowager Queen Isabella, widow of Edward II, inherited the title to their Coventry estate. Encouraged by the citizens of Coventry, she initiated a legal battle to wrest the Earl's Half from the prior and, in 1345, persuaded her son, Edward III, to grant them the right to elect a mayor as head of body governing the town (the commonalty). An agreement of 1355 signed by the prior, the town body and Queen Isabella reduced the influence of the prior to the priory precinct and a small area on the north side of the town around Bishop Street, where he had authority only as landlord. The real governance of the town now lay with the mayor and commonalty, later known as the Corporation.

We hear of places in the hinterland of the town for the first time in the twelfth century, although it appears from their Anglo-Saxon names that they had been in existence for some time. Their population had been growing and chapels were being built to serve them. Some of these can be counted amongst the earliest surviving buildings in Coventry and were to become the centres of new parishes such as Wyken. Many never acquired parish status and have subsequently been demolished – St Nicholas, north of the present town centre, Pinley and Willenhall for example. Coventry continued to prosper, principally by the manufacture and trading of woollen cloth, so that by 1280 it was perhaps in the upper teens of the largest towns in the country. By this time, urban development had extended into the Earl's Park (Little Park Street and Much Park Street), Spon Street, Hill Street and Gosford Street, which streets had all begun to fill up, while West Orchard, Well Street and Cook Street had been established off the Prior's Market and off Bishop Street.

In about 1230 a Franciscan friary, Greyfriars, was founded in part of the Earl's Park. In 1342 Whitefriars was founded on the south-east edge of the town by the Carmelites and in 1381-82 the Carthusians established Charterhouse beyond the town in open countryside. The establishment of these foundations reflects the continued and phenomenal growth in the prestige and wealth of Coventry. In 1334 Coventry was ranked twelfth in the country, equal with Salisbury, in terms of wealth. By 1377 only four towns,

London, York, Bristol and Plymouth, paid more tax. This wealth was poured into the construction of new buildings and the rebuilding of the old. Holy Trinity in the Prior's Half and St Michael's in the Earl's Half were extended to become two of the largest parish churches in the country, with spires which are still a landmark in central Coventry.

The fourteenth century also saw the emergence of religious guilds, four of which were amalgamated in 1392 to form the Trinity Guild, the most influential and powerful in Coventry. Their hall, dedicated to St Mary, was a modest building in the 1340s, which had been substantially rebuilt in stone by the early fifteenth century. The Guild also took over St John's at Bablake, established in about 1350 by one of the amalgamated guilds, St John the Baptist, with a college of priests there to administer to spiritual needs. The

The interior of St Mary's Hall, looking north to the tapestry. The scene has changed little since the original nineteenth-century engraving.

Guild, although ostensibly religious, represented the richest and most powerful merchants in the town. Their interests were closely tied with the town governing body of the Mayor and Commonalty, with whom they shared St Mary's Hall. There was only one other guild in any degree comparable. Corpus Christi in the Prior's part of the town had a guildhall on West Orchard and their adopted church was that of St Nicholas, at the upper end of St Nicholas Street. Both of these buildings have long since been demolished. A hospital dedicated to St John, with close associations with the priory, was built on marshy land in Bishop Street near the Radford Brook.

The town gaol and court were established in the fourteenth century on the corner of Bayley Lane and Cuckoo Lane, perhaps within part of the flattened site of the former castle. Gaols and castles in other towns are often closely associated. County Hall now stands on the site. Most of the nineteenth-century prison blocks at the rear were demolished nearly a century and a half ago.

In the mid-fourteenth century, Coventry was secure in its position as one of the most important medieval commercial towns in England. A gated wall was begun, encircling the town as an expression of its standing. The wall took 180 years to build, since by the late fifteenth century, due partly to the decline of the woollen cloth industry, Coventry was undergoing a period of economic stagnation. The wall was finally completed in the 1530s.

The Dissolution of the Monasteries under Henry VIII in 1539 had a disastrous effect on Coventry, made worse by the abolition of the town's most deeply rooted institutions, the religious guilds and chantries, in 1547. The priory and cathedral of St Mary formed the oldest and largest complex of buildings to be demolished. They had dominated the centre of the town for half a millennium, as long a period of time as from the Dissolution to the present day. The church might have been saved, but there was one cathedral too many in the diocese of Coventry and Lichfield. Henry VIII was far more disposed to save Lichfield, with its secular canons, than the Benedictine monks at Coventry's cathedral. Many citizens, rich and poor, must have been dependent on the ninth richest monastery in the kingdom and the disruption to the economy was enormous. Whitefriars, Greyfriars and Charterhouse were also closed down, the buildings stripped of anything valuable and then gradually taken apart. The stubs of the two western towers and the central tower of the cathedral and priory church survived for almost a century, leaving one (the future Blue Coat School) to be converted into a house. The church at Whitefriars was entirely demolished. Four church towers disappeared from the Coventry skyline, but Greyfriars tower and spire survived, joining those of St Michael's and Holy Trinity to form the famous three spires.

There was a massive sale of the confiscated monastic lands and property in the town and surrounding fields. Private individuals bought much of it: one of the most prominent of these was John Hales, a London merchant, who acquired large parts of the Priory and St John's Hospital estates. The Corporation managed to buy the land and property of the Trinity Guild, including the guildhall, the gaol and courthouse and St John's church. The guildhall acquired a new function as the town hall and the court and gaol continued as before, while no immediate use was found for the church.

Some land and property was acquired to endow new charities; Thomas Wheatley founded Bablake Boys' Hospital and Sir Thomas White provided a massive sum with which much former priory land was purchased for charitable purposes. Part of the pre-Dissolution gifts of John Bond, administered by the Trinity Guild, managed to survive confiscation by the Crown and were used to build and maintain Bond's Hospital (1570s). In his will, dated 1509, William Ford had provided for an almshouse to be built inside Greyfriars Gate. This endowment was increased by William Pisford after the Dissolution, but, unfortunately, some of the lands he purchased to support Ford's Hospital were confiscated by the Crown. The buildings erected by these charities provide today the best examples of sixteenth-century architecture in the city.

The weaving, dyeing and selling of woollen cloth had been Coventry's staple industry in the medieval period and, with some diversification into the making of caps and worsteds, continued well into the eighteenth century. Competition at home and abroad, restrictive trade practices and over-regulation have, however, been blamed for its continuing stagnation.

Coventry's independent spirit, nurtured by its struggle for self-government in the early medieval period, might explain why its people chose the Parliamentary side in the Civil War. The town was an important centre for dissent and was strongly Presbyterian. Moreover, there were no great lords resident there who could have rallied the population to the Royalist cause. The town was prepared to defend itself against attack and, for the first time, the town wall and gates were used for more than display. The town refused entry to Charles I. At several approaches, including Spon Street, St Nicholas Street and London Road, houses immediately outside the gates were deliberately pulled down to provide a clear field of fire. The displaced citizens were provided with new homes along a road in the former priory precinct. For two hundred years after the Dissolution, New Buildings was the only new development in the town. During the Civil War, Coventry's population swelled to 9,000 from the usual 6,000 and overcrowding became a problem. The redundant guild church of St John's was converted to a prison to hold captured Royalist troops and the cool reception that the captives received from Coventrians has been immortalised in the phrase 'sent to Coventry.' After the Restoration, Charles II exacted his revenge ordering that the town wall be made indefensible, leaving only the gates. The demolition was carried out over-zealously, leaving only small sections standing above ground.

Economic stagnation throughout this period meant that there was little money invested in building and the fabric of the town fossilized. In the eighteenth century Coventry was one of the best preserved medieval towns in the country. Samuel Bradford's map of Coventry, surveyed in 1748-49, shows little difference in the built-up area from that produced by John Speed about 1610. There is evidence, in fact, that the developed area had contracted along Hill Street and St Nicholas Street and on London Road outside New Gate. The construction of New Buildings was a unique occurrence. The face of the town did change, however, as medieval timber-framed buildings were demolished and replaced or simply refaced in brick, although a huge number of medieval buildings survived untouched.

Although the pace of the town's economy quickened in the late eighteenth century, the first industrial revolution based on coal and iron largely passed it by. The Coventry Canal was opened in 1769, connecting the North Warwickshire coalfield with the town, but coal was largely brought in for domestic consumption and not for industry. Connection to the canal system could do no harm, however, especially when, at the end of the eighteenth century, the network was expanded, connecting the town with London, Birmingham and Manchester.

Coventry needed new industries to achieve economic recovery. Watch-making made an appearance in the seventeenth century and, by the end of the eighteenth century, had become an important trade. In the same century an influx of French weavers led the weaving industry to turn from wool to silk and to produce newly-fashionable decorative ribbons. Together these new

The Priory Guesthouse in Ironmonger Row, demolished in the nineteenth century.

activities returned prosperity to the town. The increase in wealth did not create any new areas of Georgian terraces to reflect the age and few public buildings were erected at this time. However, increased traffic caused many of the remaining town gates to be demolished, for example New Gate, Spon Gate, Hill Street Gate and Gosford Gate. None of the Non-Conformist chapels built in this period in the town have survived.

The new industries were small scale, labour intensive and unmechanized and were squeezed into the existing urban fabric. At the end of the seventeenth century, Coventry's recorded population was 6,710. The population doubled in the first part of the eighteenth century to 12,000 in 1750 and rose to 16,000 in 1801. To the south of Coventry the rural landscape barely changed, but in Radford, Keresley, Foleshill, Walsgrave-on-Sowe and Stoke, on the north and east sides of the town, weavers' cottages sprang up and the rural population grew. These growing settlements were some distance from Coventry since ancient grazing rights on the land, known as Michaelmas and Lammas immediately around the built-up area, were jealously guarded by the freemen of the town, making them unavailable for development.

For the first half of the nineteenth century, watchmaking and silk ribbon weaving were the staple industries of the town and its northern hinterland. As both manufacturing activities needed plenty of light, but remained domestic in scale, houses with large windows on the front or back or on rear extensions became a characteristic building type. Many were being built in

A mid-seventeenth-century view of Coventry by Wenceslaus Holler.

the long medieval burgage plots, increasing overcrowding but with little improvement in sanitation. Sharp's plan of Coventry from 1807 shows a street pattern little different to that on Bradford's map of over a half century earlier. There were some new buildings around the canal basin at Leicester Row but the only development anywhere else was the re-colonization of some medieval frontages in places such as Greyfriars Green and St Nicholas Street.

The grazing rights on Michaelmas and Lammas ensured that much new development over the next few decades was located in outlying 'colonies' such as New Town, later known as Hillfields. By the 1830s, however, new building had broken the bounds of the town for the first time since the medieval period. Two new areas of development at the Butts and Queen's Road (St Thomas's) and near Leicester Row (Dog Lane) could be regarded as extensions to the old town. The latter was situated at the start of the new turnpike road to Leicester (Stoney Stanton Road, 1830-31). The former road to Birmingham and Holyhead (Spon Street/Allesley Old Road) had been bypassed by another entirely new turnpike road as far as Allesley (Holyhead Road, 1830). These improvements in communications culminated in the construction of the London to Birmingham railway line in 1838-39. The station was built south of the town beyond Greyfriars Green.

The outlier of Hillfields had been built for ribbon weavers. From the 1850s another self-contained suburb developed at Chapelfields (named after a medieval leper chapel) to house watchmakers. These specialist industrial districts, which continued to grow during most of the nineteenth century, were distinguished by their domestic scale and their large workshop windows. The factory system was almost unknown at this time and the first attempt to introduce steam engines into ribbon weaving was opposed by the weavers, who feared for their futures. Josiah Beck's factory (site today is lower Trinity Street) was attacked and burnt and the owner tossed into the adjacent mill-pool. A compromise was then introduced: weavers' houses were brought together in terraces and provided with power from a shared steam engine. The best surviving example, Cash's 'cottage factory,' was established on a greenfield site at Kingfield, well to the north of the town.

The population of Coventry doubled in the first half of the nineteenth century and stood at 36,208 in 1851 when the Board of Health plan mapped the town at large-scale for the first time. In the two previous decades new districts and new streets had been developed at an unprecedented rate, but the scale of this accurate and beautiful map shows that this new growth was grafted on to an ancient place. The pattern of medieval burgage plots can be seen over most of the 'old town' and many of the early buildings still remained.

In 1860 the removal of restrictions on the import of foreign ribbon caused the collapse of the ribbon weaving industry, which never fully recovered. This resulted in great destitution in the town and Coventry's population actually fell by 3,000 between 1861 and 1871. Watchmaking was unable to provide

Bridgeman's house in Little Park Street, a seventeenth-century house demolished in the nineteenth century.

sufficient alternative employment, despite attempts to increase the scale of production. Rotherham's on Spon Street was the only firm of any size, but did not mechanize until 1884. It was the introduction of cycle manufacture in 1869 that saved Coventry from long-term decline, launching a period of economic prosperity that was to last for nearly a century. Emerging from the earlier manufacture of sewing machines, the cycle industry developed into the production of motorcycles and motor cars and ushered in the twentieth century.

The first large-scale Ordnance Survey maps of the 1880s record the city on the eve of an explosion of unprecedented economic growth. In 1842 Coventry had lost the ancient county status obtained in 1451 and with it much of the rural area to the north. The municipal borough was more tightly drawn but still contained open land. In 1890 Radford and Earlsdon were added, nearly doubling its size. These areas were largely rural, although urban development in Earlsdon took hold slowly from the 1850s. In 1899 part of Foleshill parish and most of Stoke were added onto the north and east sides of the borough, increasing its size by another quarter to 4,147 acres. It was in this sector within the old borough that most of the physical growth of the town had taken place in the form of terraced streets of working-class housing around Stoney Stanton Road and Hillfields and around Raglan Street and Lower Ford Street to the south. Smaller pockets of more varied middle-class housing had developed east of Barras Lane, around Hill Street and Radford Road and near the railway station. In 1891 the population of Coventry was 53,000 and this had increased to 62,000 by 1901. The inclusion of rural areas within the new city boundary was undertaken in anticipation of sustained growth in the new century.

It would not be an exaggeration to state that Coventry is a twentieth-century city *par-excellence* and it is difficult to do justice to the last hundred years of its history in a few paragraphs. In the first decade the population of the town doubled to 106,431 between 1901 and 1911 (including the outlying parts of St Michael's and Holy Trinity) and reached 133,287 by 1921. Machine tool-making and component manufacture had been added to the new industries. The scale of production was also shifting from cramped workshops to purpose-built factories, powered by electricity, in the newly absorbed rural areas. The textile trade had not entirely died out and in 1905 Courtaulds established a rayon works on a greenfield site on Foleshill Road. The first nylon yarn in the country was made here in 1941. It was motor car

Christchurch, built in 1830-32, using the spire of the medieval Greyfriars church as a chancel; the church was badly damaged in 1940 and demolished after the war, leaving just the spire standing.

and cycle manufacture, however, that was to dominate the city's industry and the Coventry marques became world-famous: Eagle, Swift, Triumph, Rudge-Whitworth (cycles) Singer, Daimler, Hillman, Humber, Standard, Rover, Alvis and Lea-Francis (cars).

In 1928 and 1931 Coventry was extended by the greatest amount in its history (not including the medieval county), absorbing large rural and semi-rural areas in every direction. The area of the city in these three years increased nearly five-fold to 19,137 acres and the population, recorded in 1931, reached 167,083. Villages and hamlets at Tile Hill, Canley, Coundon, Allesley, Foleshill, Wyken, Walsgrave, Binley, Willenhall and Stivichall were to become the familiar suburbs of today. Before the Second World War, most of the housing was erected by private developers and the semi-detached house emerged as a common type, although a large amount of good-quality terraced housing was also built. Car and component factories were also constructed in the suburbs, notably on the south-west side alongside the new dual-carriageway bypass. After the Second World War, a huge amount of municipal housing was also built on cleared and bombed sites nearer the city centre and on greenfield sites at Canley and Willenhall.

The explosive growth of the suburbs continued throughout the 1930s and in 1940 the population stood at 242,000. The town centre had not been able to respond to the demands made by the increasing number of citizens and, shortly before the outbreak of the Second World War, plans were drawn up for the comprehensive redevelopment of this ancient area. Regrettably, it was decided to accommodate new shopping, commercial, administrative and educational districts in the tightly-drawn centre, with obvious consequences on the historic fabric of the ancient town. In 1937-38 three historic streets, Great and Little Butcher Rows and Cross Cheaping, were swept away for the new Trinity Street. The war itself brought huge destruction to this area, most famously the gutting of St Michael's Cathedral in November 1940. This great parish church had been elevated to become Coventry's second cathedral in 1918, 350 years after the first had been lost. The Blitz was indiscriminate in the devastation of old and new buildings but many ancient, timber-framed, buildings suffered greatly under incendiary attack.

During the war, the town centre redevelopment plans were revised to take in more of the central area and cynics have claimed that the bombing made these revisions easier. The new plans led to the demolition of many historic buildings in the post-war period. The resulting public outcry ensured that, in the 1970s and 1980s, a few were re-erected on Spon Street. The redevelopment began at the recognised historic centre, Broadgate, with the laying out of a new square, and spread westwards, creating pedestrian precincts for new shopping. The Upper and Lower Precincts gained fame for their innovative town planning and were visited by architects and town planners from all over the world. Important new buildings were subsequently erected, such as the new and third Coventry Cathedral, the Belgrade Theatre, the Municipal Swimming Baths and Coventry Railway Station. New techniques were sought in order to build as quickly as possible, particularly for schools and other buildings in the burgeoning suburbs. Coventry now boasts the longest list of post-war statutorily listed buildings outside London.

In 1951 the population of the city was 258,245, while ten years later it reached 305,060. Immigration from abroad swelled the numbers. The Irish had a long history of immigration into the city, but there were also refugees from war-torn Europe, such as the Poles and Ukranians. Immigrants from the Asian sub-continent and the Caribbean then followed and helped in the reconstruction of the city, contributing to the increasing prosperity of Coventry in the 1950s and 1960s. The population has not risen significantly since that time and now stands at about 300,000. This slowdown is largely due to the economic depression of the late 1970s and 1980s, which resulted in the closure of famous companies, such as Alfred Herbert and Armstrong-Siddeley. With the continuing decline in manufacturing, recovery, based on new service industries, has taken some time. The latest regeneration of the city is now underway, however, and, for the first time, as evidenced by the Millennium Scheme, the built heritage of the city is no longer seen as a barrier to comprehensive renewal. There is statutory protection for a good number of historic buildings (about 400) and fifteen conservation areas have been declared.

The city centre bears the strongest mark of post-war redevelopment. Historic buildings form islands, big and small, in a sea of twentieth-century development, some of which is of architectural importance in its own right. The transition from historic to modern can be abrupt, but the island that contains the three cathedrals of St Mary's, the old St Michael's and the new St Michael's is comparable to any historic area in the country. The priory and cathedral of St Mary's have recently been revealed as part of the Millennium Scheme. Over the past few decades, significant archaeology has been excavated beneath the city centre and is recognised to be of national importance. There remains much to be discovered in the future, not just in the centre, but throughout the whole city. New jostles old in Coventry, sometimes uncomfortably, but many visitors to the city are pleasantly surprised and impressed, and regret that they had not come earlier. I hope this book will aid the appreciation of Coventry's buildings of historic and architectural interest and look forward to new additions in the early years of this millennium.

MEDIEVAL BUILDINGS AND STRUCTURES

Coventry has a large number of medieval buildings, some of which rank among the most important in the country. They range from great parish churches, monasteries and guildhalls, through town gates, to the houses of merchants, craftsmen and ordinary citizens. The important buildings display a number of architectural styles, beginning with Norman Romanesque and passing through all the Gothic phases of Early English, Decorated and Perpendicular. No architects, if such a term is appropriate, are known. Humbler property in the vernacular tradition was not designed first and foremost with aesthetics in mind, it was primarily functional; this requirement, however, did not exclude decoration. The more prosperous the owners, the more they could afford and the more reason existed for display and ostentation.

The materials used for building in medieval Coventry were either the local red or grey sandstone, if the owner was rich enough, or timber-frame, usually oak. The sandstone was dug in local quarries and some of these are known: old London Road Cemetery, 'The Dell' at Barrs Hill, Radford Road and Primrose Hill Park. The oak did not travel far, probably from the field boundaries and woodland of Warwickshire. It is a myth that ships' timbers were used in local buildings. Transport costs would have been prohibitive over the ninety miles to the centre of England and timbers from dismantled ships were useless after being eaten away by years at sea.

Churches and monasteries
It is worth visiting Coventry just to see its rich collection of medieval buildings. The earliest standing structures date to the twelfth century and are

all ecclesiastical in origin. This is the period of the Norman Romanesque with typical round-headed windows, doorways and arches with thick load-bearing walls. There are no archaeological sites of earlier date that have left any traces above ground. The Roman Fort at the Lunt is just outside Coventry and is a modern reconstruction.

A small fragment of stonework of the Anglo-Saxon abbey church was probably discovered in the 1999-2000 Phoenix excavations, but this now lies re-buried beneath the newly laid Priory Gardens. The Phoenix Initiative was conceived, amongst other reasons, to excavate and permanently reveal as much as possible of the remains of the cathedral and priory of St Mary. The abbey church was founded by Leofric and Godiva in the early part of the eleventh century and, in about 1100, following the transfer of the see from Chester to Coventry, the church became a cathedral. During the following century the Normans completely rebuilt the Benedictine monastery, now a priory, as the bishop had become the abbot in title.

In Priory Gardens, off Priory Row, lie the remains of one of the oldest buildings in Coventry. This is the thick south wall (about 1.5 metres wide) of

The north-west tower of St Mary's Cathedral. Blue Coat School (1857) stands on the original thirteenth-century base.

The excavated nave of the St Mary's Cathedral with the south wall in the foreground. During the 1999-2000 excavation, 3 metres of material was removed to create the present Priory Gardens.

the twelfth-century cathedral. It stands about a metre high and the typical shallow buttresses of a Norman Romanesque church can be seen on the external face. The interior face has been re-lime-washed and a gallery of masons' marks is visible towards the west beneath the new bridge. The cathedral was extended westwards in the early thirteenth century in Early English Gothic style and fine examples of the bases of arches (responds) with shafting remain. These are attached to the interior of the west end and an opposing pair can be inspected in the room below the former Blue Coat School. The Early English north-west tower of the cathedral supports the mid-nineteenth-century school and stands over three metres in height. The corresponding south-west tower has been reduced almost to ground level, but its plan has been excavated and the new steps descend into it from the bridge. The diamond-shaped Early English Gothic pier bases that supported the nave arcade lie west of the footbridge from Priory Row to the Visitor Centre. East of the bridge the next three piers have been marked in the ground and glass cases set over them. Those on the south are rectangular, reflecting their Romanesque origins, so that in this part of the nave two contrasting styles of round arches and pointed arches unusually stood opposite each other. The two glass boxes nearest the

The Priory Visitor Centre, which has effortlessly and gracefully joined the company of the new cathedral, the spire of the old cathedral and Holy Trinity church. The architects were MacCormac, Jamieson and Pritchard, 2001.

bridge contain examples of Norman Romanesque and Gothic architecture found in the excavations on this site.

The Priory Visitor Centre, opened in 2001 in the adjacent square, Cloister Garden, contains some of the best pieces of architecture from the 1999-2002 excavations, including fragments of a fourteenth-century painting depicting the Apocalypse and a large part of a geometrically complex canopy from the pulpit in the monks' refectory.

In the corner of the next square down, Priory Place, the Priory Undercrofts can be inspected through an enormous plate-glass window. These were found in the 2000-02 excavations ahead of the building of the new cathedral office. So impressive were the remains, that the decision was made by the Millennium Project to reveal them permanently, even at the considerable expense required in redesigning the office that was to stand above them. A huge bridge structure now supports this building. Two sets of undercrofts can be seen set at right angles arranged around an external yard. Their vaulted roofs were smashed after the Dissolution of the Monasteries. They were not true cellars as the walls facing the yard formed a ground storey. The undercrofts had been built against a terrace almost 5m high. Part of this wall had been strengthened at least once and the spiral staircase that was built against it was the first part to be discovered in the excavations. Sophisticated glazed windows and a fireplace were installed in the later medieval period and are evidence that the undercrofts were converted to living accommodation. The fire may have also warmed the monks. The basic plan may date back to the twelfth century, however, including the high terrace wall at the back, although most of the vaulting dates from the thirteenth century.

The only near-complete Norman building in Coventry is the church of St Mary Magdalene at Wyken. There is a west door which is supposed to have been moved from its original location and there are the signs of blocked doorways on both sides of the nave. This is a precious survival and possibly represents the form of the many chapels in the locality that were established in the twelfth century and which have subsequently been demolished or radically rebuilt. Its form is a simple rectangle built of thick masonry. Three of the windows are typically Norman, tiny narrow openings splaying outwards on the interior to distribute as much light as possible. The tower has a Victorian pyramid top with bell openings. The only other Norman work to be seen in a standing Coventry church is in the parish church of All Saints, Allesley, where there are two round arches in the south arcade.

There are seven parish churches with later medieval work within the city boundary, two in the historic town and five in former rural parishes (Wyken, Allesley, Walsgrave, Foleshill and Stoke). The town churches of St Michael's and Holy Trinity are amongst the largest in the country. St Michael's was a cathedral for only a short time, from 1918 to 1940, but for most of its history it was the principal church of a large parish that contained

St Mary Magdalene's church, Wyken, from the north east. Note the tiny Norman window in the wall of the chancel.

the south part of the town and a considerable rural area. Holy Trinity served the north side of the town and a corresponding rural area. These large parishes had their origins in the medieval Earl's and Prior's Halves or estates. Having only two parish churches in one of the most prosperous medieval towns in the country explains their great size. St Michael's magnificent tower and spire soars to 295ft (90m), the second highest in the country, and Holy Trinity reaches 237ft (72m). Both dominate the city centre skyline from any surrounding vantage point.

St Michael's has a little Early English Gothic in the south porch and in an undercroft on the north side, but most of the church was built in Perpendicular style from the late fourteenth to the early sixteenth centuries. This is not a church, however, whose architecture is examined in minute detail by most visitors. The result of the incendiaries dropped on the night of 14 November 1940 provokes an immediate emotional response. The poignancy of the roofless walls and window tracery, overlooked by the spire, is difficult to erase from the mind. The relationship between the bombed cathedral and the new cathedral also creates a vivid impression, but helps lift the spirits. For those interested in architecture, however, there is a lot to see. The church is wide, having extended northwards with a double aisle, leaving

Opposite: The evocative ruins of the bombed cathedral of St Michael, looking east. The solidity of the new cathedral canopy contrasts with the fragility of the older walls with its window tracery.

Right: St Michael's Cathedral spire, overlooking the ruins with the spire of Holy Trinity in the background.

the spire out of centre. There are numerous chapels and altars dedicated to medieval craft and religious guilds, that must have paid for much of the later medieval rebuilding in Perpendicular style. The polygonal end to the chancel is unusual in this country but not in Coventry. St Mary's Cathedral also had this type of chancel, but with chapels built off each polygonal face. A small fragment of one of these chapels can be seen in the car park at the end of Priory Row beneath the zig-zag wall of the new cathedral.

Holy Trinity managed to survive the Blitz more or less intact and deserves to be better known. It is more cathedral-like than the old St Michael's, having a cruciform plan with the tower and spire in the centre and north and south transepts. The spire and part of the tower fell down in 1666 but were quickly rebuilt. The oldest part of the church appears to be the north porch, which is thirteenth-century Early English Gothic in style and vaulted. The porch wall into the north aisle could, however, be older and contains the roughest stonework in the church. In the twelfth century the

Above left: Holy Trinity church from the west, with tower and spire rising majestically from the centre.

Above right: The Early English Gothic church of All Saints, Allesley.

Chapel of the Holy Cross is known to have lain in the churchyard, but its position is uncertain. As in St Michael's, most of the architecture is Perpendicular in style, ranging from the second half of the fourteenth to the early sixteenth century. The nave has a magnificent timber roof and over the central crossing arch is a newly restored Doom painting, a rare survival. Below Marler's chapel, on the north side of the chancel, there is a charnel house full of human bones disturbed by grave digging. The exterior of the church was much restored in the nineteenth century, and, unfortunately, the architects Rickman and Hutchinson used Bath stone, which is an alien material in sandstone Coventry.

All Saints' in Allesley is Coventry's best example of an Early English Gothic church, although much restored in 1863 by the architect James Murray when the chancel was rebuilt. The tower is also Early English, the only one in the city. The spire is a little later. The church has more presence from a distance than within the village.

St Mary's, Walsgrave-on-Sowe (formerly Sowe), sits in a more prominent but noisy position overlooking a dual-carriageway. It has an Early English chancel with typical Y-tracery, but then displays all the medieval Gothic styles with a squat, Perpendicular tower and Decorated-style nave arcades.

St Lawrence's, Foleshill, lies isolated in the extensive parish that had no obvious village centre. It can be easily missed travelling along Old Church Road. The tower is Perpendicular but taller and more elegant than Walsgrave's. There is not much more medieval work to be seen, the remainder having been

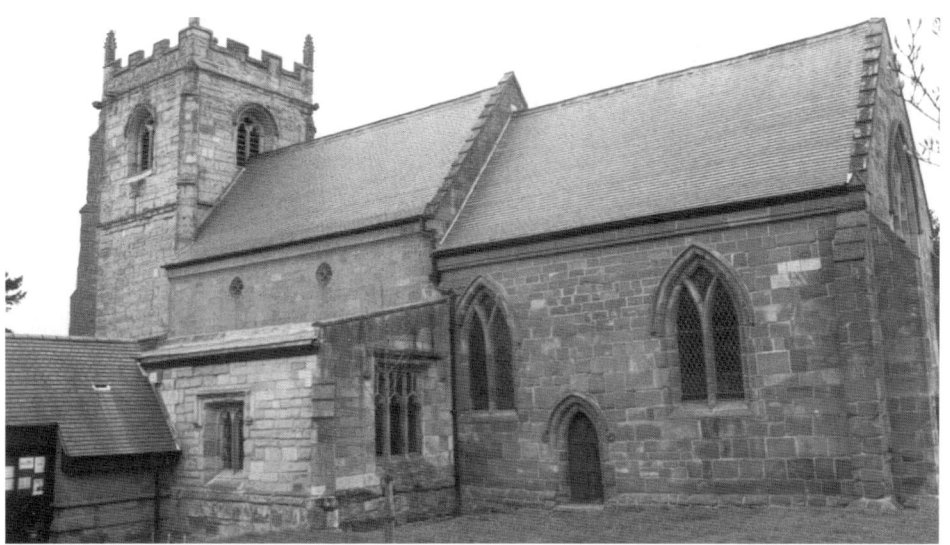

St Mary's church, Walsgrave (on-Sowe) from the south.

St Lawrence's church, Foleshill, from the east, with its unusual grouping of extensions.

Above: The collegiate and guild church of St John the Baptist.

Left: St Michael's church, Stoke, from the south west, dominated by its Perpendicular Gothic tower.

Opposite: The chapel of the medieval hospital of St John, better known as the Old Grammar School, sorely in need of a new use.

rebuilt at least twice in the nineteenth century, partly in brick. A strange chancel 'wing' of 1927 lies on the south side, at right angles to the normal east-west orientation. Inside there are cast iron piers in the nave.

St Michael's, Stoke, stands isolated in its parish where, as in Foleshill, there was no established village centre. This is the third of Coventry's Perpendicular Gothic towers attached to a small rural church and, except for the Decorated south aisle, it has little else that is medieval. The enlargement dates from 1861 and is by James Murray.

The other medieval churches in Coventry were built for a variety of reasons and are located in or near the old town centre. St John the Baptist's, dominating the entrance to Spon Street, was established in the mid-fourteenth century by Queen Isabella as a chantry for, amongst others, 'her late dear lord' (she had deposed her husband Edward II and had him murdered). It also served as the church for the Guild of St John the Baptist which, in 1392, was united with three other guilds to form the Trinity Guild. The church is cruciform in plan and appears superficially to have been built to a single scheme; closer examination, however, reveals anomalies and changes of plan. The south aisle with its late fourteenth-century Decorated windows is out of step with the later south transept and nave clerestorey. Much of the fabric appears to be of fifteenth-century date, although the church was heavily restored by Sir George Gilbert Scott between 1858 and 1877. The elegant tower has distinctive round corner turrets at parapet level (bartizans). A college of priests lived in a building on the north side of the church which became a prison (the Bridewell) after the college was dissolved in 1547. This was demolished in the nineteenth century. The church was used as a prison for Royalist troops in the Civil War and only became a parish church, the third in Coventry, in 1734.

The Old Grammar School, on the corner of Bishop Street and Hales Street, is in fact the chapel of the medieval hospital of St John, founded in the twelfth century and rebuilt in the fourteenth century. It was closely associated with the Priory of St Mary. Two blocked arches can be seen on the exterior, which led into the south aisle, now demolished; there are two corresponding blocked arches on the north side leading into the north aisle. The hospital beds were normally placed in the aisles. The hospital was dissolved in 1545 and the land sold to John Hales, who had promised Henry VIII to re-endow some of it to provide a school. Hales set up the first school in Whitefriars church, but the establishment was probably moved in 1557 to the former hospital chapel along with the choir stalls to serve as benches. Remarkably, the medieval stalls have survived but carry the scars of many centuries of subsequent use by schoolboys.

The ruins of the Chapel of St James and St Christopher, hugging the side of Spon Bridge.

It was not until 1572, however, that the school was formally endowed with the land promised. In this year Hales's successors granted part of their estate to the Corporation to oversee 'one perpetual free-school'. The school moved to new premises on Warwick Road in 1885 (King Henry VIII). The old building is in desperate need of a new use.

The tiny Chapel of St James and St Christopher sits like a sentinel on the town-side of Spon Bridge. It was in existence from at least 1395 and may have been founded by Coventry weavers with the interests of wayfarers in mind. Apparently avoiding the confiscations of the Dissolution, it remained in the hands of the weavers, later the clothiers' company, and may, by the late eighteenth century, have been converted to a dwelling. Although ruinous in 1761, views from about 1800 show it being used as a house again. The Corporation purchased the building in 1936 with a plan to preserve it but the war intervened. After minor bomb damage, the chapel was allowed to become ruinous again and the restoration scheme was dropped. Stripped of its roof and accretions, only the sandstone walls of the chapel now stand. Further out, beyond Spon End, was a lepers' chapel and hospital, situated on the out-of-town corner of Hearsall Lane and Allesley Old Road. The chapel managed to survive into the early nineteenth century as an agricultural building but was then demolished. It gave its name to the watchmaking quarter of Chapelfields.

The Greyfriars or Franciscan friary was established in the 1230s and Christchurch (Greyfriars) spire is all that remains. The third of Coventry's famous three spires, it stands 230ft (70 metres) high and dates from about the mid-fourteenth century. Originally standing between the nave and the chancel of the church, its position was typical of friary churches, as was its octagonal shape. The church was demolished after the dissolution of the house in 1539.

The architects Rickman and Hutchinson added a new church, known as Christchurch, in Early English style in 1830-32, using the space under the tower as the chancel. This explains the presence of Bath stone at the lower levels of the walls. The church was badly damaged in 1940 and was demolished in 1950. The spire is now used as a café.

In 1342 a second friary (Whitefriars) was established on the south-east approach to the city by the Carmelites, but here it is not the church spire that has survived, as at Greyfriars, but the red sandstone two-storey east range of the cloister. It contains a cloister walk and rooms, including part of the chapter house, on the ground floor and a dormitory on the first floor. The stone vaulted cloister walk is an impressive space and the dormitory above is an even larger room with an exposed tithe barn-like timber roof that traditionally was supposed to have been reused from an agricultural building after the Dissolution. Recent tree-ring dating has confirmed its medieval date, but using

The sole remains of the Greyfriars church, Coventry's third surviving medieval spire, also known as Christchurch.

35

Whitefriars – the surviving east range of the cloisters with a late sixteenth-century oriel window inserted into the dormitory above.

timber felled in 1475 and 1493-94. The roof could either have been constructed in 1493-94 in one phase, reusing the earlier timber, or have been constructed in two phases nearly twenty years apart. The house of the Whitefriars was surrendered in 1538 and John Hales subsequently acquired the property and converted it into his private residence, known as Hales Place. The bay window on the west side of the dormitory, along with other stone-mullioned windows, probably date from this phase. The church was used as a school for a short time but was eventually demolished. The walls, excavated in 1961-64, lie on the north side. From 1801 the buildings became part of a large workhouse complex. These later buildings have in turn all been demolished, but the surviving monastic east range lies uncomfortably close to the 1960s Ring Road. Until recently, the Herbert Art Gallery and Museum operated the building as a branch museum and archaeological store, but public access has unfortunately now ceased. The transformation of the immediate area to the east by Coventry University may provide hope for a new use for this rare survival.

After Mount Grace in Yorkshire, Charterhouse in Coventry is the second-best preserved Carthusian monastery in the country. It was founded beyond the confines of the town in 1381 and the area still retains a semi-rural character. What survives is a part of a stone range, which contained the prior's lodging to the south and a room open to the roof, the monks' refectory,

The Charterhouse from the garden on the east side; one of Coventry's most important medieval buildings.

immediately to the north; this was located over a ground-floor room. A floor has subsequently been inserted so that the original carved tie beams of the roof are now seen in second-floor rooms. Here in the corridor is a reused oak doorhead from one of the monk's cells, the only one surviving in the country. The two parts of the building were divided by a stone wall and a medieval wall painting of the crucifixion is preserved on the north side of this wall. An inscription dates it to the time of William Soland, prior from 1411 to 1417. Only the lower part of the painting survives below the inserted floor. The north end of the building is timber-framed throughout and dates from the sixteenth century. The monks' cells were located in a cloister on the east side of the building in an area demarcated by stone walls, now a garden and bowling greens. The church, excavated in 1984–87, was situated on the north side of this area and the present stone wall running east from the building is on the line of the south church wall. The most impressive monastic precinct wall in Coventry is to be found at the Charterhouse, running to the east of the main building for a considerable length. It is topped by a characteristic steeply-pitched coping. To the north, the wall turns west and then south to reach the bridge over the Sherbourne, close to the site of the former water-mill of Bisseley. The Charterhouse is used by Tile Hill College as a training centre.

37

Manors, houses and cellars

There are the remains of two medieval manors in Coventry. The town was extending southwards in the early thirteenth century, enveloping the site of the castle and part of the park. The Montalts had inherited the Earl of Chester's estate in Coventry and Cheylesmore Manor was established by them in about 1250 to replace the castle of the former Earls. The new manor house stood overlooking the reduced park. Queen Isabella succeeded to the manor of Cheylesmore in about 1330 and Cheylesmore was thereafter a royal property. This connection inspired the motto on the Corporation coat of arms – *Camera Principis*, the Chamber of the Prince. Edward, the Black Prince and Isabella's grandson, became owner of the manor, a royal scion destined never to be king. The town wall was built in the second half of the fourteenth century uncomfortably close, actually destroying some of the manorial buildings and separating them from the park. In the sixteenth to eighteenth centuries, there were a number of complicated leases to the Corporation. Finally, in 1819 the Prince Regent sold the manor to the then tenant, the Marquess of Hertford.

Only the gate house, that led into the manor complex from the town, and two cross-wings have survived. Part of the solar wing, with an impressive crown post roof, was unfortunately demolished in 1957. The present building is timber-framed but was almost entirely covered in render before restoration took place in 1966-68, directed by F.W.B. Charles. The building was converted for use as the Registry Office. The oldest part of the frame is in the cross-wings. The east wing dates from the fourteenth century and has a much

Left: Cheylesmore Manor – the gatehouse (fourteenth and fifteenth century), now the city's Registry Office.

Opposite: The sole remains of Caludon Castle (fourteenth century). This is still surrounded by an impressive moat.

restored crown post rafter roof visible in the room on the first floor. The wall frame is the simplest with large braces strengthening the corners. The west wing was probably constructed in the fifteenth century and has a close-studded (vertical posts at close intervals) wall frame. The three-bay gate house with the gateway in the centre is also close-studded, but has been dated to the sixteenth century. In 1968-70 the modernist Registrar's Office was attached to the west wing. The whole complex, old and new, is hidden away behind a taller office block fronting New Union Street, creating a typical Coventry island of history.

By contrast, little survives of the stone-built Caludon Castle. The remains can be seen in a municipal park and stand prominently on a grassy platform surrounded on all sides by a moat, the north side much broader and perhaps designed to function as a fish or mill pool. Two bays of the north wall of the hall range stand two-storeys high. The building is of grey sandstone with window and door reveals picked out in red. The upper hall storey is nearly twice the height of the undercroft storey below. There is no sign that the undercroft was vaulted and the hall probably had a timber floor. A shaft belonging to a chimney stack runs within the thickness of the wall between the two bays. The ground level appears to have been raised as the window cills are now at ground level. This may be demolition rubble. A geophysical survey of the platform revealed a clear plan of the walls belonging to the remainder of the buildings.

It is not known exactly who built the small surviving part of the hall of Caludon Castle. John de Segrave obtained a license to crenellate in 1305. The manor passed to his daughter Joan and her husband, John Mowbray, in 1353. A year later they were granted another license to crenellate. The hall, which is in Decorated Gothic style, was perhaps built not long after, preceding on less grand a scale the great hall at Kenilworth Castle (*c.* 1390). With the loss of almost all the buildings before they could be illustrated, it is difficult to judge how much they were intended to be a castle first and a residence second. In the fourteenth century there was less need for feudal lords to defend their home. It is likely that Caludon Castle resembled more the crenellated hunting lodge of Weoley Castle in Birmingham than the great stronghold at Kenilworth.

There is a roofless stone house in Much Park Street, which only re-emerged into view in 1940 when the street was bombed during the Blitz, the later brick buildings which had previously enveloped it having collapsed away. It is a good example of a medieval first-floor house with the principal chamber above and a stone vaulted undercroft below. Dating from perhaps the late fourteenth century, it is rectangular in plan with two bays turned at right angles to the street and set some way back from the street frontage. The north wall has almost entirely been lost, providing a good view of the interior and the scars of the

The Stone House, Much Park Street – a view through the missing north wall.

The Lych Gate Cottages – early fifteenth century – with the 1857-extension to the right and the 1938 mock timber-frame at the rear.

stone vaulted cellar. The south wall contains a fireplace, which is corbelled from the exterior face. Nothing is known about the history of the house and who owned it in the medieval period. It is a sophisticated building, and was probably owned by a wealthy merchant, but this is only speculation. It is interesting that the building is set back from the historic street frontage and it has been suggested that a timber-framed two-storey shop was attached to the stone gable facing the street. It now stands on a grassy bank enclosed by the modernist buildings of Coventry University.

The other surviving medieval houses in Coventry are all timber-framed. The three-storey, jettied Lych Gate Cottages in Priory Row have only recently been identified as early fifteenth century as a result of tree-ring dating. They were originally thought to have been post-Dissolution in origin. The timbers in the building were, however, felled in 1414–15 and were probably used soon after in the building when 'green,' as was the usual practice. Felled oak hardens quickly and becomes unworkable. This date would make this the only surviving priory precinct building in Coventry. It was situated in the forecourt of the cathedral overshadowed by the now lost south-west tower (see in Priory Gardens

Left: The building at Nos 114-115 Gosford Street, one of the earliest timber-framed buildings in Coventry (fourteenth century).

Opposite: No. 169 Spon Street, one of the oldest semi-detached houses in the country, built as a pair (fifteenth century).

adjacent). The construction of the building would have required the demolition of the forecourt wall and this is curious. The building faced into that part of the churchyard where funerals entered, hence its name (OE *lic-* corrupted to *lych* – corpse). There appears to be no form of heating, which in this period would normally have been a fire in the centre of a hall, the principal living room. It is possible that the hall or halls were in a wing at the rear, leaving the three floors on the front for another use, perhaps linked to the administration of the priory or even let for commercial use as shops and storerooms.

An earlier building, dated to the fourteenth century by its distinctive crown post roof, lies in Gosford Street (Nos 114-115) and has been recently converted into a pub (its new name, Whitefriars, has no known historical association with the building). The building has thankfully not been over-restored and originally consisted of a two-bay hall, which subsequently had a floor inserted, creating two rooms. This was a frequent occurrence in the sixteenth century, when chimneys began to contain the fire and halls fell out of fashion. The room upstairs, open to the roof, forms the upper part of the medieval hall. The frontage is a hybrid, neither preserving the later shop front or restoring the original frame. The pub is gradually building up a clientele for its authentic atmosphere and a fashionable 'make-over' should not be encouraged.

The most convenient place in Coventry to study medieval houses is Spon Street, part open-air museum, part commercial street. Here, from 1969 to 1990, some but not all timber-frame buildings that had been threatened by development elsewhere in the city centre were dismantled and re-erected. Spon Street had managed to escape both serious war-time damage and post-war redevelopment and contained a good number of historic buildings in its own right. About half the timber-framed buildings have been moved into the street and the others are *in situ*, although not all are medieval in date.

The building at No. 169 can claim to be one of the oldest semi-detached houses in the country. This caused some amusement and argument when published in a book of *Notes and Queries* some years ago. This is a genuine Spon Street pair, probably dating to the fifteenth century. Each probably used the ground floor as shop or workshop; the function of the chamber on the projecting jetty above is not known. At the back each house had a hall, providing the main living area, but these have been demolished.

Further west along the same side of the street is another building original to the street in the form of a terrace, numbered 159-162. This is an intriguing example of a 'Wealden' (rural Sussex) house adapted to a town situation. There are two halls situated directly at the front and they are charac-teristically recessed with small angled braces in the top corners of the

Above: Nos 159-162 Spon Street – a good example of the Coventry version of the Wealden house. The two-storey windows mark the position of the halls.

Left: Nos 163-164 Spon Street, a three-storey merchant's house transported from Much Park Street in the 1970s.

Opposite: Nos 1-2 Spon Street, Wealden-type houses (note the recessed halls) dating from the fifteenth century and re-erected here in 1989, the last to be moved.

overhanging eaves. The hall on the extreme left formed a single unit with the two-storey jettied bay next door. The next two bays are two storey, also with a jetty, and it is likely that the hall for this house was situated at the rear, as in the pair at No. 169. The terrace continues by repeating one more time the same sequence of hall and three-jettied bays.

Other buildings of interest here include the large house at Nos 163 and 164 Spon Street. This was dismantled and moved from Much Park Street in 1971-74. It introduced a different house type to the street since its size and three-storey height was more typical of the merchants' houses in Much Park Street. Spon Street, by contrast, was an artisan suburb, whose houses tended to be only two storeys. The last buildings to be re-erected in Spon Street were, in 1989, Nos 1-2. They are another good example of the Wealden type with the recessed halls and corresponding tall windows. Tudor House (Nos 14-15, latter half of the fifteenth century) bears little resemblance today to photographs of the Recruiting Sergeant pub of a century ago. It was restored in 1977 and 1985 and contains a recessed hall in the centre with two flanking jettied and gabled cross-wings. The curved and cusped (scalloped) wind braces in the roof of the present shop are well worth seeing and indicate that this was one of the highest quality buildings in the medieval street.

Tudor House, 14-15 Spon Street (fifteenth century), unusual in having gables facing the street on either side of the hall.

Nos 20-21 Spon Street (fifteenth and sixteenth century) re-erected from Much Park Street.

No. 9 Spon Street – (fifteenth century), re-erected from Much Park Street.

There are several other medieval buildings worthy of attention in Spon Street, most of which are *in situ* and have been altered. As a result they are more difficult to recognise as dating from this period.

In Upper Spon Street (Nos 119-124) at the corner with Barras Lane, west of the Ring Road, is a row of medieval houses which was originally intended to be removed to Spon Street. By 1990 the attitude on the moving of buildings had changed; it is now thought that a building should not be divorced from its archaeological and physical context. It is also accepted that timber-framed buildings should no longer be restored to their original form but have the alterations of later periods also preserved in their own right. A Buildings Preservation Trust was set up in the mid-1990s to restore the buildings *in situ*. At the time of writing, due to its good efforts, the restoration of two of the six houses in the terrace has been completed according to current conservation principles. These are rather compact medieval examples with the hall at the front and an interior 'jettied' chamber occupying part of the hall space at the rear.

A great many medieval houses, particularly of the merchant class, had stone cellars, some with stone vaults. A number have survived, though access to them by the public is difficult. The easiest one to visit is situated below the 1990 Tourist Information Centre in Bayley Lane. This area was badly

No. 16 Hinckley Road, Walsgrave, one of the oldest houses in Coventry with a rare cruck-frame within and a similarly rare thatched roof.

damaged in the Blitz and many of the medieval buildings were lost. The cellar fortunately survived and was restored as part of the new Tourist Information Centre. It is an impressive two-bay stone rib-vaulted structure with a narrow pedestrian doorway alongside a broader 'goods entrance'. There are other good survivals along Earl Street and High Street and the location of many more is known but not their present state of preservation.

There are a few medieval houses in the suburbs, the best examples being a fourteenth-century cruck-framed house on Hinckley Road at Walsgrave-on-Sowe, beyond the parish church. Galveston Cottage on Coundon Green has managed to hang onto a single cruck frame. Pickford Farm in rural Allesley has the form of a medieval farmhouse with a hall and two cross-wings, but the left-hand side cross-wing and hall have been rebuilt in brick.

St Mary's Guildhall

One of the most impressive cellars or undercrofts in Coventry forms part of a building which should not be missed on any visit to the city. The Guildhall is one of the most important medieval buildings in the country but, curiously, relatively unknown. Most of the building we see today was built between 1390 and 1425 for the new Trinity Guild, uniting four earlier guilds. The large rib-vaulted undercroft, broad enough to need piers in the centre, supports the lofty and stone-built hall above. This has a magnificent timber roof and a profusion of colourful angel bosses. At the upper (dais) end of the hall is one of the many treasures – a tapestry dating from about 1500, celebrating the visit of Henry VII and his queen to the hall. The window above had to be reduced to accommodate it. At the opposite (lower) end is a timber minstrels' gallery, below which are three doors traditionally leading to a buttery, kitchen and pantry. Today the central door still connects to the kitchen, but the other two rooms are now known as the Old Council Chamber and Prince's Chamber, each with a very different *décor* and ambience. The Old Council Chamber leads to a room in the stone Caesar's Tower, probably the Treasury (Latin: *Tresoria*), which still contains the Corporation chest for valuables. The tower was badly damaged in the war and rebuilt. The rare medieval kitchen is currently hidden from view by post-war alterations, but there are plans to remove these and restore the kitchen to its former glory. It will then be accessible to visitors.

St Mary's Guildhall – the north front (late fourteenth-early fifteenth century). The lower part of the window was blocked by a tapestry made in about 1500, which still hangs in its original position. The small windows and doorway at ground level formed the front of a cellar tavern.

Status and defence

It took about 180 years, between the mid-fourteenth and the early sixteenth centuries, to build Coventry's town wall. It was clearly, therefore, not primarily a defensive feature and should be seen as having symbolic value, representing the 'coming of age' of Coventry as an important medieval town. Twelve gates were eventually erected and the circuit of the wall measured 2.25 miles (3.6 kilometres). King Charles II ordered that the wall be made indefensible as punishment for the refusal of Coventry to admit entry to his father in the Civil War. Much of the wall was subsequently demolished but, even in its degraded form, it was still a major feature in the topography of the town in the eighteenth century. The gates were preserved until the late eighteenth century when all but two were removed.

The best preserved part of the wall, standing up to 3 metres (10ft) high, runs between the two surviving gates, Cook Street Gate and Swanswell Gate. In the 1930s Lady Herbert's garden was laid out along this section. It was endowed by Sir Alfred Herbert, the head of the famous machine tool company,

Cook Street Gate (fifteenth century), restored in 1918; a view from within the wall.

Swanswell Gate, earlier Priory Gate (fifeenth century), situated on the private road that led out of the priory precinct. The arch was blocked in the nineteenth century to make a dwelling.

in memory of his wife. Cook Street Gate was in existence by the early fifteenth century. It stands at the upper (north) end of the wall on a relatively minor public road, which led towards Harnall. The gate, which had been used as a dwelling in the nineteenth century, was presented to the city in 1913 and restored in 1918 when the crenellations were added. It has an open arch and carries the distinctive scar of the town wall facing into the garden.

Swanswell Gate, by contrast, has its road arch blocked. This was originally the private gate (Priory Gate) from the precinct of St Mary's Priory to its orchards outside the wall and estates further out at Harnall. It replaced an earlier gate when the prior convinced the Corporation to enclose his fishponds within the new wall. The town wall east of Swanswell also acted therefore as the boundary wall of the extended precinct. The construction of Hales Street in 1850 bypassed the gate and allowed it to be used as a dwelling, hence the blocked arches. The door from the original room over the gate onto the town wall can be seen in the garden. The scar of the section of the town wall that continued eastwards can be seen on the opposite side of the gate facing Hales Street. Appropriately, accommodation at the gate is currently

Whitefriars Gate (fourteenth to sixteenth century) was probably only a single screen wall when first built; it was converted into a gatehouse in the later part of the sixteenth century.

used by CV One, the Council-sponsored company that secures and maintains the public areas of the city centre.

Other parts of the town wall and towers can be seen off Lamb Street, the east side of Upper Well Street, off Lower Holyhead Road, near Parkside and between Cox Street and Gosford Street beneath the Ring Road flyover. Gates and sections of the wall have been marked at Hill Street, Spon Street and Queen Victoria Road, Shelton Square, Bull Yard and Gosford Street/Far Gosford Street. A further section of town wall has recently been identified at Bond's Hospital, contained within a later garden wall.

Whitefriars Gate, now a toy museum on Much Park Street, dates from about the mid-fourteenth century. It was probably constructed originally as a single stone arch, leading to the Whitefriars monastery, perhaps on the site of a house plot. A vaulted gate proper was situated nearer to the friary buildings and was reached directly from the London Road before the town wall blocked the way in about 1430. When John Hales took over the buildings in the mid-sixteenth century, he probably had another wall built parallel to the original arch and a room slung between the two. This explains why the timber-framed room projects below the arch and why there are no

St Catherine's Well, Beaumont Crescent (fifteenth century). It was probably the well head of the water supply to St Mary's Priory or another monastic house in Coventry.

stone side walls. The structure borrowed the timber-framed walls of the neighbouring houses. The one on the right is hidden behind the brick wall and buttresses erected in 2001.

Wells

There were many public wells and conduit heads in medieval Coventry, but none have survived in the city centre. There is an intriguing conduit head (St Catherine's Well) in Beaumont Crescent, off Holyhead Road about a mile from the centre. It consists characteristically of a small stone-built chamber with a steeply pitched stone roof, which would have covered the spring head. Many similar well heads survive elsewhere in the country associated with the water supply to monasteries. It is possible that St Catherine's Well was a source of water for St Mary's Priory. This would have entailed the laying of lead pipes for some considerable distance and included the crossing of the River Sherbourne, south of Spon Street. Using only gravity and the contours of the land, water could have been directed to the cloister of the priory where another conduit head would have been situated, distributing water to the rest of the buildings.

SIXTEENTH- TO SEVENTEENTH- CENTURY BUILDINGS

The Perpendicular Gothic style died out during the sixteenth century under the influence of the European Renaissance. At first the imported classical architecture was 'impure', adapted to English buildings that had continued to develop their own Tudor and Jacobean style. In the Palladian designs of Inigo Jones, Classicism finally arrived in the early seventeenth century.

Economic decline meant that much of the classical revival bypassed Coventry. Relatively few new buildings were erected and most of these continued the timber-framed tradition. For those willing to pay, however, an increasingly sophisticated exterior decoration was employed. Bridgeman's house on Little Park Street (see page 18) was one of the finest examples of this type, but was demolished in the early nineteenth century. Nevertheless, in the same century, Coventry's decorated houses of this period became a serious object of study (See A.W. Pugin, *A Series of Ornamental Timber Gables*, 1839).

Institutional

The complex around Bond's Hospital and Bablake forms one of the finest islands of history in the city centre. Bond's Hospital was endowed under the will of Thomas Bond (*d.* 1506) as an almshouse and occupies the northern side of a secluded courtyard and a considerable frontage on to Hill Street. It is not certain whether the intended 'Bede House' for ten men and a priest was quickly established, for the present building was described as newly built in 1581. Most of Bond's Hospital is of timber-framed construction with a profusion of close studding on two storeys. It is likely that the original arrangement had individual cubicles on the ground floor and a communal room on the first floor with a fireplace. The end bays beyond the two cross

Bond's Hospital (late sixteenth century), an almshouse displaying a profusion of timber and which has been altered many times over the centuries in response to new needs and standards.

passages probably housed the kitchen, housekeeper's and master's chambers and a chapel. The building was extensively restored in 1832-34 and in 1846-47 by Thomas Rickman and H.W. Hutchinson. Many of the features of the building date from this period, including the first-floor bay windows and elegant chimney stacks and pots. Both floors were converted to individual rooms with fireplaces. The street frontage was extended north with a new gable built against the remains of the town wall, which can be seen in the side wall beyond the door. The elevations here are rendered.

New pots have recently been placed on the stacks, replicating lost nineteenth-century examples. In 2004, to conform with higher standards demanded for sheltered accommodation, the building will again be re-ordered internally, doubling the space allocated to each room.

Bablake School is housed in buildings originally occupied by a medieval college of priests attached to St John's church. Thomas Wheatley founded the school for poor boys in 1560 and the east range of the college was taken over to accommodate it. Mostly of square panel frame construction, the two-storey building stretches over a considerable distance between Hill Street and an internal courtyard. Apart from the central section, which contains an

Above: Bablake School (fifteenth-sixteenth century). The hall is situated in the centre and is an impressive space. The courtyard side of the building has a very different appearance.

Left: Ford's Hospital (sixteenth century) – a magnificent example of a profusely carved timber-frame almshouse. The small courtyard within is a delight. (Also see frontispiece).

impressive hall, possibly of fifteenth or early sixteenth-century date, much of the building appears to date from modifications to the school from the mid-sixteenth century onwards. The street frontage has a sandstone ground storey and a shallow projection reflects the location of the former late medieval hall. Although the whole length is jettied, the beam ends in the centre support only a gallery in the hall and not a whole floor. The courtyard frontage has a first-floor gallery above an open ground-floor walkway or 'cloister'. The porch and gable are nineteenth century in date. In 1890 the boys moved to the present site on Coundon Road and in recent times the old school has been used as an office. The mock timber-framed building on the opposite side of the courtyard is the Bablake old boys' club, originally the offices for the school foundation (1898).

Ford's Hospital stands alone in timber-framed splendour in the hinterland of the present city centre on Greyfriars Lane, once the main route to Warwick via Greyfriars Gate. It was founded by William Ford in his will of 1509, which provided for an almshouse to be built near Greyfriars Gate. The building was erected by Ford's executor, William Pisford, who increased the endowment to cater for six couples and a priest. This is one of the better known of Coventry's timber-framed buildings and its renown is justified by the profusion of close-studding and the rich carving on the frame and barge-boards. It is two storey, with a central passage from the street through the front range, running into a small, tightly enclosed courtyard, from which four doors lead into the almshouse accommodation. The first floor projects on a coved jetty, making the courtyard even more confined. This space is one of the delights of historic Coventry and is worth a few moments' study and contemplation (see frontispiece). Originally, the accommodation was located on two floors but, with changing needs over the centuries, much of the original internal arrangement has been altered. The almshouses were badly damaged in the war but were thankfully restored.

Houses

There are no surviving great houses from the sixteenth and seventeenth centuries. One of the largest, New House, at the junction of Sadler Road with Keresley Road, was built in 1586 by John Hales, nephew of John Hales, but was demolished in 1778.

The houses still in existence are domestic in scale. In the city centre they are timber-framed. The three-storey Golden Cross on the corner of Hay Lane and Bayley Lane, dating from the late sixteenth or early seventeenth century, was much restored in the nineteenth century. It has close-studding on the upper floors and moulded jetty boards, but without tree-ring dating it is difficult to know how much of the timber-frame is original. Its finest feature is the 'dragon beam,' visible in the ground-floor ceiling. This a large timber beam that enables a jettied first floor to pass round a corner building.

Further along, on the opposite side of Hay Lane, seventeenth-century timber-framed buildings are masked by later brick frontages, typical of the way in which many Coventry buildings were adapted. The timber work can be seen on the end gable of the house adjacent to the Council House Gate or by taking the passage into Castle Yard and observing the rear. These buildings were restored in 1990.

On leaving Castle Yard via the Bayley Lane entrance, one passes by a richly carved, timber-framed building known to many as Browett's (No. 22 Bayley Lane) which, after a century as a solicitors' office, is now available for a new use. The timber-frame has survived best on the first floor and is richly decorated on the thin posts attached to the frame, the heads of windows and panels, the barge boards and the corner post. There is a dragon beam on the interior. This house may have its origins in the rebuilding of a medieval house known as 'Castle Bakehouse' in the early fifteenth century when it belonged to St Mary's Priory. Bayley Lane probably runs through the bailey of the twelfth-century castle and the remains of bread ovens were excavated in Castle Yard in 1990.

The building at No. 16 Spon Street was moved from 142-143 Spon Street in the early 1970s. It represents the last stage in the long timber-frame

Above left: The Golden Cross (sixteenth to seventeenth century), an impressive, though much restored, three-storey house obscured by a vicious outbreak of hanging baskets.

Above right: No. 22 Bayley Lane (sixteenth to seventeenth century). Some magnificent carving in timber has managed to survive on this corner leading to Castle Yard.

Above: To the right is No. 16 Spon Street (seventeenth century).

Right: The Old Windmill, Spon Street. This is a good example of how many of the timber-framed buildings in Coventry were obscured by later alterations.

tradition in Coventry, when skills were declining. The restoration has produced a curious building with new square panel frame interrupted by a simple shop window. The roof trusses are of the greatest interest.

Further west along the same side of Spon Street is the Old Windmill which, along with others in the street, gives a good idea of how the appearance of timber-framed buildings was changed over the centuries. Its alterations include rendering over the timber, the insertion of windows without respecting the frame and the use of a board to hide the projecting jetty. As there is no trace of a hall, this building has been dated to the sixteenth century. There is a later brew-house preserved at the rear. It has been a tavern for many years ('Ma Brown's') and is a favoured place for its historical atmosphere.

In rural houses stone seems to have been used as frequently as timber. There was a plentiful supply at the dissolved Coventry monasteries. Stivichall Grange, Lonscale Drive, is a misnomer as it lies in Kingshill in ancient Stoneleigh Parish and was never a monastic grange. The building is three storeyed with two rooms on each of the floors and stone-mullioned windows. It had an unusual plan, with an entrance to what were probably the principal rooms at first-floor level from a porch, now removed, on the high bank alongside. The former staircase tower, which ran through all floors, has been absorbed into the extension at the rear. All three floors and their rooms were heated by chimneys on the gable ends. This was not a farmhouse and its original function is unknown; there is an obvious display of ostentation. The building was severely vandalized in the 1970s, and during this time and subsequently, in the conversion to the present flats, many original features were lost.

The Stone House in Allesley, overlooking Birmingham Road, has a date stone of 1608, which on this building might be trusted. The initials W.W.C. suggest it was built by father and son, William Clark, who purchased the house that year. This is a substantial village house of two storeys with an almost centrally placed two-storey porch. On either side are tall gables and the windows are mullioned

Stivichall Grange with its unfortunate twentieth-century extension in brick to the right and rear.

Above: The Stone House, Allesley (seventeenth century), a fine example of symmetrical frontage. The turnpiking of the road left the pavement at a higher level.

Right: The Smithy, Stivichall Croft (seventeenth century) – a typical example of the central lobby-type house of this period.

on the first floor and mullioned and transomed on the ground floor. This house reflects the new internal arrangement of the time – without halls, floored throughout and with rooms heated by chimneys. The near symmetry also reflects the adoption of classical fashion in the middling order of houses.

In Stivichall Croft symmetry had caught on at the Smithy, a mid-seventeenth century brick house with stone-mullioned windows, which survive on the side elevation, but have been lost on the front. The plan is of

Manor House Farm, Henley Road, a surprising survival in urban Coventry.

the typical central-lobby type, with the front door entering a small lobby with doors to the two rooms on either side and the base of the chimney opposite. The centrally placed chimney allowed both rooms to be heated by a single chimney stack. It rises through the house to heat the first-floor rooms and then terminates in three diamond-shaped chimney stacks.

Manor House Farm on Henley Road, on the opposite side of Coventry at Wyken, is a timber-framed house of seventeenth-century date. Its most distinctive feature is the massive brick chimney attached to the exterior of the frame and not integral to the plan. The house was extended in brick during the eighteenth century.

In Tile Hill, No. 12 Station Road is also timber-framed, but appears to have been built in two stages, the elaborate diagonal pattern being later, perhaps early seventeenth century, and typical of town housing. Ivy Farm House, in Ivy Farm Lane, Canley hamlet, is a good example of sixteenth- or seventeenth-century square panel framing. The charming Broomstick Cottage, off Woodway Lane, Walsgrave, is one of only three surviving thatched houses in the city.

EIGHTEENTH-CENTURY BUILDINGS

It is only in the eighteenth century that Classical architecture could be said to have arrived in Coventry. However, there were few opportunities in a town that was only just beginning to revive economically. Due to an outbreak of dry rot, the third Drapers Hall, designed by Henry Couchman in Palladian style, did not survive long into the nineteenth century and was replaced by the fourth and present Drapers' Hall, another study in pure classicism. County Hall, Cuckoo Lane and St Bartholomew's church, Binley, are the best surviving examples of eighteenth-century classical architecture in the city.

Coventry has no Georgian squares and crescents and for much of the period the fashionable domestic style was manifested in a few individual but very stylish town houses, a good many more modest houses and the façading of timber-framed buildings. The latter was not straightforward, as the proportions of Georgian domestic architecture did not easily fit the squatter storeys of medieval houses. The look of the town was also changing, as the timber-framed tradition declined and brick was more frequently used. The local clays produced a rich orange-red brick with an attractive texture. These bricks had for some time been replacing the timber and mud panels in earlier timber-framed buildings.

Ecclesiastical

The medieval church of St Bartholemew, Binley, was unusually demolished and replaced in 1771-73 by a church in classical Palladian style. The work was undertaken by the Craven family, lords of Binley, who at this time were reorganizing the park at Combe Abbbey under the guidance of Capability Brown. It has, however, been suggested that the church was designed by Henry Couchman. The church is built of high-quality ashlar, very tightly coursed. The main entrance is at the west end and displays the usual Classical motifs of pediments, round arches and Tuscan columns. There is, however, another doorway on the north side of the building under a porch supported by two columns. This was private, leading first into a windowless vestibule and then into the Craven family chapel. The exterior of the church itself is plain, almost severe, with plain round-headed windows. The chancel is a small semi-circular apse. There is an octagonal bell-turret with a *cupola*, immediately behind the west façade. The interior decoration is, by contrast, a riot of showy plasterwork. The private Craven chapel is separated from the main body of the church by an alabaster screen. Close by is Binley Vicarage, an amalgam of many styles from the seventeenth to the nineteenth century.

No other Anglican place of worship was built in this century. The only Non-Conformist chapel to survive to the present time is the much altered Foleshill Congregational (now United Reformed) chapel at the junction of Foleshill Road and Old Church Road.

St Bartholomew's church, Binley, from the south west. Another door on the north side leads into the Craven family chapel.

County Hall (1783-84), Cuckoo Lane, and the brick-built Prison Governor's House, Pepper Lane. This is Coventry's finest eighteenth-century public building, recently repaired on the exterior.

Institutional

The most important public building of the eighteenth century is County Hall, the exterior of which was recently refurbished after many years under protective netting. At the time of publication the interior awaits a new use, having been empty since the new County Court was opened in Much Park Street in 1989. The building consists of two distinct parts, the red-brick prison governor's house fronting Pepper Lane and the stone courtroom facing Cuckoo Lane. The courtroom has a new stone pediment (2000) supported on four Tuscan columns. The 'ground storey' consists of four blind arches while a fifth arch to the right serves as the main entrance. The prison governor's house is, by contrast, constructed of brick with a timber pediment applied to the third storey. The courtroom was designed by Samuel Eglinton and erected in 1783-84; the house may have been built with the new gaol (1772-74). The adjacent prison was rebuilt after 1831, but was largely demolished about thirty years later for the new library (1867). Two blocks of Edwardian buildings, one containing a courtroom, were built on the prison site, completing two sides of a central court, which was used as a prisoners' exercise yard.

The courtroom is an impressive space with a coved ceiling springing off an elaborate dentilled cornice. Some of the original late eighteenth-century fittings have survived, particularly in the gallery, but most of the furnishings, including the judge's bench, date from a refurbishment in the 1840s. Over the judge's bench is a magnificent royal coat of arms. The prison governor's house was also refurbished at this time, when the staircase was replaced. The Victorian postbox on the side of the house was restored a few years ago.

The building stands at the highest point in central Coventry and may lie over the motte of the twelfth-century castle. A goal and courtroom are known on this site from the medieval period and are well documented for several centuries.

Houses

The best row of Georgian houses can be seen in Priory Row, which provides a fitting backdrop to the cathedrals' area. The interior of No. 9, closest to the new cathedral (the Dean's House), was badly damaged during the Second World War, but its façade survived. This is one of the three, high-quality, early eighteenth-century town house façades in Coventry. It is built of brick on three storeys with good detailing. Giant fluted Ionic pilasters, a heavy cornice and a fine doorway dominate the composition. The rest of the houses in the row (Nos 7-8) are considerably plainer and are late eighteenth or even early nineteenth century in date. John Gulson, the well-known philanthropist, lived at No. 7. The houses possess another layer of interest by being positioned over

No. 9 Priory Row (the Dean's House) – giving no hint of the serious damage suffered by the interior during the Blitz. It has the best eighteenth-century front railings in Coventry.

Nos 7-8 Priory Row standing over the buried remains of the Cathedral of St Mary. The Millennium Scheme is visible to the left.

the crossing and chancel of St Mary's Cathedral. No. 8 contains a warren of cellars that may relate to the cathedral foundations, while Nos 7-8 have the two south piers of the central crossing tower lying beneath a later rear extension.

The two other good early eighteenth-century town houses are in Little Park Street. Kirby House, at No. 16, was damaged in the war. Most of the house had managed to survive, albeit in a parlous state. After much delay, it was extensively rebuilt in 1981 but the original façade was fortunately retained. It is brick-built, three storeys in height with four giant Doric pilasters and a good central doorway. The visible boxes of the sliding sash windows betray their early eighteenth-century date. The detailing on the façade is worth some attention. The interior staircase has survived and has fine twisted and fluted balusters.

Towards the Council House is the best preserved of the three early eighteenth-century houses. No. 7 Little Park Street was built around the 1720-30s for a silk merchant. It has six giant Corinthian pilasters rising from a deep plinth. The narrow central doorway and the window above with its decorative surround is similar to that at Stoneleigh Abbey, designed by the Smith brothers, William and Francis, in 1720-26. There is an unproven tradition that the brothers also designed this and the two other early eighteenth-century town houses. To the left, behind a new 'terrace' and steel canopy, is the much less elaborate extension that was used as a silk warehouse.

The interior of No. 7 has survived more or less intact and has a good turned baluster staircase and panelled rooms on the first floor. In the late 1990s, after standing empty for a number of years, the building was converted

No. 7 Little Park Street, originally a silk merchant's house and warehouse. Now it is a pub, mis-titled 'The Varisty'.

into a pub, but it was impossible to incorporate the main rooms of the house without substantial demolition. These were set aside for staff accommodation, except for one panelled room which, with the silk warehouse and a new extension, became the public area. The brewery could not be convinced to use the silk merchant's theme for the new name.

Beyond the city centre, eighteenth-century houses are concentrated in the north west in the village of Allesley and in the farmland that stretches to the city boundary towards Meriden. This is good evidence for the considerable wealth that was accumulating in the area at this time. Lion House and Park House, Nos 87-89 Birmingham Road, are good examples of a spacious and lofty pair with an unusual plan. On the opposite side of the road a row of houses (Nos 50-60) provides an attractive mix of vernacular architecture. They are perched above the roadway on a raised footpath caused by the turnpiking of the road in the 1820s and the removal of gradients. These elevated footways are a distinctive feature of the village. The houses continue around the corner along a narrow alley in a mix of timber-frame and brick of various dates.

Three large but separate houses have a broadly similar appearance. The two-storey Lodge, 40 Birmingham Road, is early eighteenth century in date, with dormer windows and two brick pilasters on corners of the frontage. Arden House, 74 Birmingham Road, is three full storeys in height and of a similar date but has later bay windows on the ground floor. Wigan House, 71 Birmingham Road, dates from the mid-eighteenth century but its sash windows have been replaced.

Foleshill Mill House, off Alderman's Green Road, is the only surviving dwelling associated with a water mill of which over twenty are known to have operated within the area of the city. It is a tall, two-storey brick house with later features such as the ground-floor bay window and the decorated barge boards. A few years ago the derelict water mill opposite the house was demolished and a terrace of houses built over the site in a rough approximation of the form of the previous mill.

Industrial

The arrival of the Coventry Canal (1769) was followed by a new building type – the canal warehouse. A fine example was squeezed between the canal on one side and the new road to Leicester (Leicester Row) on the other, so that the goods could be easily transferred from one mode of transport to the other. It appears that warehousing began at the north end and spread southwards and down the slope of Leicester Row towards the terminus of the canal. The first

The canal warehouses, Leicester Row. The earliest warehouses in the row (late eighteenth-early nineteenth century) dominate the picture.

section was not originally roofed. It has three arched openings, each of which led to narrow loading bays. The recessed half arches flanking these openings were designed for holding the open gates. This pattern of doorways was repeated in the two-storey building adjacent and appears to date from the late eighteenth or early nineteenth century. By 1807 the canal warehouses were already the impressive length we see today (130 metres or 426ft – the same length as the cathedral and priory church of St Mary's), but the lower half was then rebuilt in two stages with additional storeys. The red-brick section dates from the nineteenth century and the lowest part, with concrete lintels and frame, from 1914. The large doorways along the street frontage all lead directly to the canal side where loading bays, or *lucams*, protected the transfer of goods and contained cranes.

Today all of the canal side is protected by a canopy, which forms an integral part of the roof of the lower and older warehouse at the upper end. In the high retaining wall on the opposite side of the basin are two large brick vaults (*c.* 1853) for storing coal in the dry, destined for the gas works in Abbotts Lane. A few years ago they were converted into a restaurant (now a nightclub), obscuring the original fabric. Several new buildings were erected at the basin in the 1990s and the last one will be completed in 2004.

Communications

Spon Bridge has been in existence since the thirteenth century, but it appears that it was substantially remodelled in the 1770s using stone from the demolished Spon Gate. It consists of three round arches between four three-sided buttresses. The Drapers Fields bridge near the canal basin dates from about 1770, but the parapets have been extensively rebuilt.

The bridge at Whitley used to carry the main road to London, before the present route opened in 1830. It has four three-sided buttresses, with half-domed caps flanking the broad round arch emphasized by *voussoirs* and a large keystone. Whitley water corn mill stood on the south-west side of the bridge, but it was the last of a long line of buildings stretching back to the medieval period, and it was demolished in 1955. A bungalow now stands in its place.

Nineteenth-Century Buildings

An accelerating pace of growth, after three centuries of economic stagnation, is reflected in the number and variety of new buildings constructed in this period. With the growth of the town came new institutions, all needing to be accommodated. New churches were erected to serve the growing population. For the first time industrial buildings of all scales form a distinct and prominent group. New materials were introduced, such as terracotta, highly-fired blue bricks, cast iron, steel and concrete. It is easier now to identify the architects of buildings, for, during this century, they finally emerged as a separate profession from among the ranks of masons and builders. Building records are also more abundant, particularly later in the century, when plans had to be submitted for approval to the local authority.

The century is renowned for its varied architectural styles, beginning with Georgian and Regency based upon Classical motifs. The fashion for facing brick gave way to rendered surfaces, but only for the most expensive of houses. The ascent of Victoria to the throne in 1837 was soon followed by an architectural free-for-all, where earlier styles were revived, adapted, tidied and mixed together. Eclecticism was only one response. Victorian architecture tried everything: Gothic, the vernacular of timber-framing, Tudor, Jacobean, Italianate, Renaissance and Neo-Classical – both Greek and Roman. This profusion of styles was mostly limited to principal buildings in Coventry; however, the styles spread to humbler dwellings through decoration. Business and commercial premises and industrial buildings began to acquire architectural expression from the mid-century.

Ecclesiastical

St James's church, Stivichall, was an ancient parish church entirely rebuilt in 1817 at the expense of the Gregory family, lords of the manor. The new building was designed by James Green and is constructed in stone. It has a tiny chancel with a ribbed vault and an aisle-less nave, both with strong exterior crenellation. In 1955 a new church was built with emphatic pointed Gothic gables and the 1817-nave became the chancel.

Anglican churches were being established to serve new congregations in the growing suburbs. St Peter's church (architect Robert Ebbel) was

Opposite above:
St James's church,
Stivichall, part built in
1817, extended in 1955.

Opposite below: St Peter's,
Hillfields (1840-41) an
austere brick
Commissioners' church,
recently saved from
demolition.

Right: St John the Baptist's
church, Westwood Heath.

constructed in 1840-41 for the new parish of Hillfields. It is a typical Commissioners' church – an austere aisle-less brick hall with a Perpendicular tower. The high outer wall is regularly interrupted by tall lancet windows between even taller buttresses. The interior is a single space with an impressive gallery on iron columns and single-span roof trusses that conceal cast-iron tie beams. A few years ago the body of the church was threatened with demolition, the shrinking congregation having moved to a new 'worship space' adjacent. The old church, one of only two listed buildings in Hillfields, was fortunately saved, but it may undergo major internal changes for conversion into flats.

St Mark's on Stoney Stanton Road, opposite the Coventry and Warwickshire Hospital, was consecrated in 1869 to serve the adjacent community to the north (architects Paull and Robinson). With a distinctive Gothic exterior of rough-faced sandstone, the interior was partially hidden some years ago by being converted to a clinic and only the bottom of the round columns of the nave can be seen. There is an unexpected surprise through a doorway off the clinic – the full height of the chancel with a great painting of the Resurrection by Hans Feibusch on the west wall (1962-63).

St John the Baptist's at Westwood Heath was built in 1842-45 to a design by Scott and Moffatt. Pevsner identifies the architect as Sir George Gilbert Scott and the church as 'one of the first archaeologically conscientious churches in the country'. What is meant here is that the church was not designed to a standard pattern, providing maximum space for fast-growing

Above: St Thomas's church, Keresley, from the south.

Left: St Thomas's church, Longford, from the north west.

suburban congregations, but with an effort to recreate the medieval village church. St John the Baptist is small and simple with a nave, chancel and bellcote but not quite authentic, as the windows all have the same pattern of tracery, unlikely in an ancient church. It is interesting that the parish that it served did not relate to Coventry but to a new rural parish in the north of Stoneleigh.

St Thomas's, Keresley, was consecrated in 1849 (architect Benjamin Ferrey). This was to serve the growing population in the rural areas to the north of Coventry. It has an aisle-less nave and chancel, akin to the Commissioners' churches, but a substantial tower and broach spire (octagon rising out of a square base) as compensation. The later three-gabled extension on the north side has overbalanced the original design. The rural aspect of this church has somehow managed to survive to the present day.

A much later Gothic town church (1874) was built in Longford in a more populous urban district north of Coventry. St Thomas's (architect J. Cotton) is red brick with stone dressings and is situated on a busy road. There is a tower on the north-west side with a squat spire. St Andrew's by S.S. Teulon in Church Lane, Upper Eastern Green Lane, was built at almost the same time (1875). It is also Gothic with a north tower and forms an interesting grouping with the vicarage and school. Coventry has not quite reached this spot and it remains peacefully rural in its cul-de-sac lane.

By the mid-nineteenth century Coventry had long outgrown its parish graveyards. The main design of the new municipal cemetery opened in 1847, now known as London Road Cemetery, was by Joseph Paxton, an enlightened choice. His assistants must have helped with individual buildings such as the Anglican and Non-Conformist chapels. The Norman Romanesque chapel for Anglican burials was given the most prominent position on the edge of a refashioned medieval quarry. The tower, with its pyramidal roof, emphasises the elevated location. The choice of style was deliberate, as was the selection of Neo-Grecian for the Non-Conformist chapel. This building, by further contrast, sits in a more secluded and lower position at the far end of the cemetery and is half hidden amongst the trees. Here we have a temple façade with columns and pilasters supporting a pediment, flanked by low pavilions, now roofless. The chapel is badly in need of repair, but an alternative use is difficult in this setting.

The secular buildings in the cemetery are notable and include the Italianate Lodge and house for the cemetery superintendent, the octagonal Prospect Tower in similar mode (substantially restored in 1995-96 by the

The Norman-Romanesque Anglican chapel, London Road Cemetery, with an unexpected rose window in the west-end gable.

The Non-Conformist chapel, London Road Cemetery. A new use is desperately needed but none is obvious.

Above left: The Superintendent's Lodge, London Road Cemetery.

Above right: The Prospect Tower, London Road Cemetery, repaired in 1995-96. It once commanded a view over the Sherbourne Valley.

City Council's conservation team), the raised promenade walk and boundary wall and the Gothic monument to Joseph Paxton. None of these are a surprise once it is understood that it was Paxton's intention to create not only a burial ground for the dead, but a park for the living to enjoy. There was no other formal park in the city at this time. London Road is one of the most important Victorian cemeteries in the country, not only for its architecture but also for the clever use of abandoned medieval stone quarries and for its fine new planting.

Many of the city centre Non-Conformist chapels have been demolished, some as a result of war damage. The survivors date from the late nineteenth century and are more prone to be decorated or even adopt a traditional style than their predecessors of a century earlier. An example on the fringes of the centre is the early 1880s Baptist chapel in Queen's Road (architects, G. and I. Steane of Coventry). It is Gothic and a free interpretation of the Perpendicular style (note the Decorated rose window). It is built of red brick with a sparing use of stone dressings. The front is asymmetrical with a square tower on the east side that was severely truncated in about 1987, after much controversy.

The Baptist chapel, Queen's Road. The tower was once much taller.

Above left: The Congregational chapel, Warwick Row.

Above right: St Osburg's church, Hill Street. This is Coventry's first Catholic church after the medieval period.

Left: The Salem Baptist chapel, Lady Lane, Longford.

Closer to town, G. and I. Steane designed an unexpectedly elaborate Renaissance-style Congregational chapel on Warwick Road (1891). Like the Baptist chapel, it is built of brick but the stone dressings are profuse and richly moulded. The imposing façade is flanked by two octagonal, domed towers, but a 1960s vestibule detracts from the composition. Current plans for remodelling the church include its removal. Inside there is an impressive gallery.

The Salem Baptist chapel on Lady Lane, Longford, is by contrast an austere building with little external decoration. The first chapel was built in

1765 and there were rebuildings in 1807, 1825 and finally in 1872. The main body of the chapel is a brick rectangle, three 'storeys' high, with rendered pilasters on the bay divisions. The 'pedimented' east-facing front, containing the main entrance, is reached by a flight of steps from the street. The chapel has the usual gallery. Part of a possible earlier chapel, rendered and painted white, is attached to the end facing west.

Two Catholic churches were built in Coventry, the better known being St Osburg's situated in a prominent situation on Hill Street. It was the first to be erected (1843-1845) using the unusual material of granite rubble, although the details are in cut stone. It is a generous church, which was apparently inspired by German and Belgian models seen during a tour of the continent by the architect C.A. Hansom and William Ullathorne, leader of the congregation and later R.C. Bishop of Birmingham. A tower and spire of the broach type, added a few years later, sits on the south-west side with an aisle running from it almost the full length of the church. The east end of the chancel faces the road.

St Mary and St Benedict's was opened in 1893 on the corner of Raglan Street and Hood Street. It is Early English in style, built of brick and stone dressings. The modern vestibule entrance, replacing an earlier one, obscures the west end of the church and provides an architectural counterpoint to the Gothic interior of the main church.

Institutional

Drapers' Hall on Bayley Lane, opposite the bombed cathedral, is one of the finest Neo-Classical buildings in Coventry. It was designed by Thomas Rickman and H.W. Hutchinson in 1831-32, the fourth building on the site. The first Drapers' Hall stood next to the Drapery in the late medieval period, a long double row, probably timber-framed, consisting of stalls and shops running from Bayley Lane to Earl Street. St Mary Street was constructed along its line in about 1863.

The site of Drapers' Hall was then surrounded on three sides by buildings and Classical architecture was a solution to the problem of lighting the intended principal rooms. In classical Rome or Greece many buildings were top lit to keep rooms cool and in Drapers' Hall there are roof lanterns and windowless walls. The room at the front was converted into a library in 1890 and windows inserted into the wall. This spoilt the symmetry of the façade,

Draper's Hall, Bayley Lane. The façade once had five Corinthian columns but three were removed to make way for the windows. There are magnificent rooms within.

which originally had five Corinthian columns and a blind door on the right-hand side to balance the working door on the left. All the main rooms have walls decorated with pilasters and cornices with magnificent Classical detail in plaster, wood and stone. The main door is reached by a steep flight of steps so that the ground floor is well above street level. This allowed the construction of a complex of cellars, which were necessary to store large quantities of food and drink, since the Drapers' Company was by this time essentially an exclusive wining and dining club. There are late nineteenth-century extensions on the south side in stone and red brick, which contain offices, one of which has two curious curved doors. The building was used in 2000-01 as a temporary centre for Holy Trinity church, but new uses, which include public access, are now being sought.

The growing city needed more council office space and, in 1863, a red sandstone extension was built on the east side of St Mary's Hall. It was designed by James Murray in a late medieval style. The principal frontage is on Bayley Lane, but it also turns the corner into the new St Mary Street, laid out on the site of the former Drapery. Murray's work effortlessly blends in with St Mary's Hall and provided the cue for design of the new Council House earlier in the next century. The building also contained a police station and cells.

James Murray also designed the new Blue Coat School in a Gothic *château* style, which was erected in 1856-57. There had been a school off Priory Row

Left: The Council House extension 1863; the three pointed windows light a large room, representing a medieval hall.

Below: The Old Blue Coat School, now Holy Trinity church centre, Priory Row. It proudly announces the beginning of the Millennium Scheme.

since the early eighteenth century, accommodated in the remains of the north-west tower of the Cathedral of St Mary's and in some later extensions. Murray had just completed the restoration of the Lych Gate Cottages next door (1855), inserting the brick ground storey and adding the tall brick chimneys (page 41). During the construction of the first part of the school, the remains of the west end of the cathedral were discovered and these were dug out and deliberately left exposed in recognition of their antiquarian interest. The first phase of the school building contained a covered playground and kitchen on the ground floor and a schoolroom open to the roof above. Murray wished to keep as much of the medieval tower as possible, but only the base survives to a height of about 3 metres (10ft), with a few pinnacles of stone above. Murray's elevations are capped by a roof of steep pitches and cones, resolving the complex shape of the medieval tower. The tower contained the matrons' room and dormitories. The school prepared orphaned girls to enter domestic service at sixteen, but, by the end of the century, it was only in use as a home, with education provided locally by council schools. The girls left during the Blitz in 1940, never to return.

The building was thoroughly restored and repaired in 1999-2000 as part of the Millennium Scheme. It provides an imposing backdrop and gateway to the newly laid out public gardens and squares. Restricted access has been provided to the medieval part of the tower (thought to be a former chapel) below the school, which was originally reached through a tall arch from the north aisle of the cathedral. The plate glass windows on the ground floor reflect the location of the original unglazed openings of the playground and the leaded lights mark the position of the kitchen. On the façade new scupltured heads, each a member of the project team, replaced the completely worn and unrecognizable original versions.

The Tudor style of building was considered appropriate when the two ancient schools in Coventry decided to leave their buildings for new premises on the edge of the then city. King Henry VIII School on Warwick Road (1884-85), successor to the Old Grammar School, was designed by Edward Burgess. The two-storey buildings front Warwick Road and are built of red brick with stone dressings. A tower marks the entrance with an octagonal turret attached to the north-east corner. The south end of the building, near the junction with Spencer Avenue, is three storey in height with tall square, rather than octagonal, chimneys. It contained the boarders' dormitories and the extensive masters' accommodation. A variety of buildings have subsequently been added over the years, those at the rear being of least architectural interest.

In 1890 Bablake School moved into new buildings arranged at right angles to Coundon Road, leaving a large open area in front of the school. They are

King Henry VIII School, Warwick Road.

Bablake School, Coundon Road.

in the Tudor style with stone detailing, mullioned bay windows, steep roofs and the obligatory tower. This marked the main entrance as was the convention but, in contrast to King Henry VIII school, the composition on either side is more regular. As at King Henry's, there have been many new

Spon Street Junior School (Spon Gate) in Upper Spon Street.

buildings added over the intervening years, cramping the site, the most recent being the primary school in contrasting modern style.

The Tudor style was also used in the municipal sector at the end of the nineteenth century. Spon Street Junior School, Upper Spon Street, was opened in 1890-91 to the rear of the original school of 1871, demolished in the 1970s. It is built of warm red brick with large stone-mullioned windows. The school incorporated a house at the east end for the mistress. The roofs are an eclectic mix of gables and hips with a crenellated frontage running between the separate girls' and boys' entrances. The buildings were saved from demolition a few years ago, but they are not currently in use as a school.

Houses

No large mansions were built in Coventry during the nineteenth century, although Whitley Hall, renamed Whitley Abbey, was partly reconstructed after a fire in 1874. It was demolished in the 1950s. Several large 'gentleman's residences' were constructed in the rural hinterland for those who had prospered from the revival in Coventry's fortunes. Although many did not survive the expansion of Coventry, a number, such as Stoke House, Copsewood Grange (James Hart, ribbon manufacturer) and Coundon House (Caldicotts related by marriage to the Waters family, wine merchants) still stand within undeveloped or much reduced green areas. Others lie on the edge of the built-up

Coundon Court from the south; it was built in 1890-91 for the cycle manufacturer, George Singer. The house has much florid internal woodcarving and plasterwork.

area such as Keresley Grange (Rotherhams, watch manufacturers), Coundon Hall (Illiffes, publishers), Coundon Court (Singer, cars), Keresley Hall (Hillman, cars) and Keresley Manor. The names reflect the pretensions of the owners; none were connected with monastic granges or manors. Ancient names could be taken from one area and applied in another. Keresley Grange is in fact in historic Coundon. Some of these houses have changed their original names, e.g. Coundon Hall is now the Old Hall Restaurant, Keresley Hall has been renamed the Royal Court Hotel and Keresley Grange is simply called The Grange.

The architecture of these buildings is for the most part conventional, reflecting some of the shifts of fashion that occured in the Victorian era. Stoke House and Coundon House are stuccoed with classical details, while the houses of the late nineteenth century reflect, but not very strongly, the Arts and Craft movement, which gave rise to a successful style in neighbouring Birmingham and elsewhere. The reintroduction of brick with stone dressings in loosely Tudor or Jacobean style was treated with restraint, even austerity, but in compensation the interiors can be quite sumptuous, as at Keresley Manor and Coundon Court, for example. There are relatively few houses with mock (planted) timber-framing, such as Keresley Manor, Keresley Hall and The Chace, London Road.

Bird Grove on George Eliot Road, formerly fronting Foleshill Road, is a stuccoed house of the early nineteenth century. Enveloped by industry and

The Chace, Willenhall, built in 1897 for Charles Iliffe, city coroner and poor law director, was converted into a hotel in 1930.

Bird Grove, George Eliot Road; once a rural retreat, the original house in which Eliot lived is to the left.

housing during the early part of the twentieth century, it has suffered over the years. The street name betrays the historical connection between the house and the famous local author. George Eliot lived in the house from 1841 to 1849 when it was surrounded entirely by fields and overlooked a stream valley, which now forms a dip in the road. Eliot lived in the left-hand side of the building, where the original entrance, with a porch, is situated. About ten years ago, after decades of neglect, a refurbishment for new community uses saved the building. In visual terms, however, the restoration was not entirely successful.

The new professional classes settled in more modest but fashionable terraced houses surrounding Greyfriars Green immediately to the south of the town. The Quadrant on the east side of the Green was completed by 1863 and is an elegant curved terrace of stuccoed houses, displaying a profusion of Classical motifs but with little attempt at symmetry, that being no longer the order of the day. Bay windows, back in fashion after decades of flat Georgian sashes, enliven the frontage and are a good marker for the early decades of the Victorian era.

On the opposite side of Greyfriars Green is an earlier and less integrated row of Georgian and Regency Houses, in both brick and stucco and with considerable variations in height. The terrace was, unfortunately, broken into two by the building of Greyfriars Road in the early 1970s. Many of the houses have had shops inserted into the ground floors, but with little *finesse*. Some of the best examples are without shops as, for example, the elegant 26 Warwick Road with Corinthian pilasters and a balcony supported on open-lattice iron columns, or the red brick and more restrained former Reform Club at No. 5 Warwick Row.

In the second half of the nineteenth century, the middle classes settled not only on the south but also on the west side of the old centre and terraced streets of modest but comfortable houses developed in the area between Spon End and Radford Road, taking advantage of the release of Lammas land. A great variation in style was used, but the bay window predominates, the earlier houses being stuccoed, as in Middleborough Road. The fashion for public parks also developed in the Victorian period and it is no surprise that one was established in this district. Naul's Mill Park was laid out at the end of the century around a pool that formerly fed a water mill. The circular

Above: The Quadrant, Greyfriars Green, a splendid curve of stuccoed town houses with no attempt at symmetry.

Right: 26 Warwick Road – unspoilt by unsympathetic shop fronts.

The Old Post Office, Longford.

bandstand, *de rigeur* at the time, was unfortunately demolished many years ago. Although the general appearance of the area has not changed significantly, the cumulative effects of 'improvements,' such as the profusion of new metal and plastic widows, can spoil an historic area. This was newly declared a Conservation Area in 2003.

Well beyond the city centre in Longford is an example of a modest but well-preserved house (*c.* 1820-30) known as the Old Post Office (there is an old shop front in one corner). It is square and symmetrical, built of red brick with the principal frontage arranged sideways onto the road. Here a porch on two columns announces the main entrance, which used to overlook a much larger garden.

Industrial

This is the first century in which industrial buildings dominate. They reflect the old and new industries in Coventry and, in particular, the attempts of the ribbon industry to adapt and survive. The new cycle and car industries did not leave a distinct building type, most production taking place in north-lit sheds in a variety of sizes, most of which have been demolished. The office blocks built on the street frontage by the larger firms are often the most architecturally interesting buildings. Multi-storey factories were relatively rare in Coventry's industrial history, though a number have survived.

Most weaving and watchmaking took place in purpose-built family houses where a room, the 'shop', was set aside for the work and provided with a large window. The weavers' shops were most often located on the upper storey of the main house, hence their name – 'top-shop.' Watchmakers worked in a rear wing, or on the first floor of a three-storey house – hence, 'middle-shop'. These were invariably placed in the rear of the houses, so that from the front the buildings look like any small villas of the period, perhaps deliberately so. A trip down the entry (covered alley) is necessary to discover the rear workshop. If the shop was located in a wing, then this could reflect master rather than journeyman status and the longer the wing, the more prosperous the master. In contrast, weavers' shops needed windows on both sides of the house to light the loom. Weavers' 'top-shops' are therefore usually visible on the street frontage.

Vast numbers of these houses have been demolished, but an almost complete watchmaking quarter has survived in Chapelfields, dating from the late 1840s. Many of the significant architectural details, such as the multi-pane workshop windows, sash windows, door cases and slate roofs, are now missing. Fortunately, sufficient 'unimproved' buildings survive for visitors to be able to appreciate their original appearance. Good examples of watch-makers houses in their original state (a dying breed) can be spotted by walking the streets of the district. The houses on Allesley Old Road (Nos 21, 23-9, 31, 49) belonged to the wealthier masters and are therefore larger, more architecturally showy and with longer 'top-shop' wings, which could contain

No. 31 Allesley Old Road – an unusual two-storey workshop that belonged to a master watchmaker.

Nos 26-27 Spon Street, originally a small house in the centre, it was extended to either side by Rotherams, the watchmakers.

Left: Nos 67-72 Far Gosford Street: ribbon-weaving 'top-shops' in much need of a restoration scheme.

Opposite: Cash's cottage factory, Cash's Lane, now housing association flats.

an office. Were it not for the misguided home improvements carried out since the 1960s, Chapelfields would be one of the most important historical quarters in the country.

A row of watchmaking 'top-shops' can be seen closer to town in Lower Holyhead Road, which was shortened by the construction of the Ring Road in the mid-1960s. There are more on Norfolk Street and Gloucester Street, off Barras Lane, and a late example at No. 31 Hill Street.

Watchmaking on a larger scale took place in a much extended Georgian house in Spon Street (Nos 26-28 Spon Street, Rotherhams), to which were added wings at the rear where steam power was introduced in 1884. Eventually, a workforce of up to 500 was employed here. The original house is in the centre, with a more elaborate door case and a brick-face less glazed than to the left and right.

There are far fewer ribbon-weaving 'top-shops' surviving, an isolated example being a row of six in Far Gosford Street (Nos 67-72), which have suffered from unsightly alterations. The 'top-shop' windows are in both the rear and front elevations. Much of nineteenth-century Hillfields was devoted to the trade, but was comprehensively redeveloped from the late 1950s causing mass demolition, including the famous Eli Green's Triangle in Brook, Vernon and Berry Streets. A row survives in Charles Street opposite St Peter's church. There are examples of 'top-shops' in Longford in Hurst Road where the workshop windows have been unsympathetically altered.

Steam power was only applied to ribbon weaving with any frequency from the 1840s. Some works were organized as factories, with employees receiving weekly wages, but none of these have survived. The great resistance by the home weavers of Coventry to mechanization led to the creation of hybrids, which permitted the workers varying degrees of independence. In 1856-57 John and Joseph Cash, who were benevolent Quakers, established their 'cottage factory' at Kingfield, now Cash's Lane. The essence of the scheme was a row of weavers' cottages with living accommodation on the ground and

first floors and with 'top-shops' above. At this level the looms were powered by shafting running through each of the shops and connected to a steam engine, but each weaver worked independently, paying rent for the house and power. Two rows of these cottage factories were built, one along the road and the other beside the Coventry Canal, although more were intended. They are brick buildings of some architectural distinction, with mock-timber gables marking the end of the row and a centrally-placed arch for the vehicular entrance into the rear yard. The 'top-shops' are spacious with tall windows, usually divided into double-arched multi-pane lights. The scheme was dealt a bitter blow by the collapse of the ribbon trade in 1860. The individual 'top-shops' were then connected together to form a single factory space and the weavers became factory employees. Ribbon weaving ceased long ago and today the two Cash's buildings are owned by a housing association, which converted the 'top-shop' storey into two rooms by inserting a floor and repartitioning.

Another type of hybrid more closely resembled a factory, for here the weavers did not live on the premises. The factory on New Buildings was built about 1849-50 with a steam engine on the north gable, powering a corn mill at the north end of the building and looms on the two upper floors. These floors have the characteristic large multi-pane workshop windows on both sides. The looms were rented to independent weavers and probably worked for no more than a decade before the trade collapsed in 1860. Following this, the building was used as a 'Ragged School' and a drill hall. After 1850 a house was built on to the south gable, probably for the factory owner or supervisor. It later became known as the Armoury.

The factory building has a three-storey elevation in one direction, once facing into a rear yard, but now onto the Millennium Cloister Garden and Visitor Centre, and four storeys on the street frontage, the ground storey here consisting of a series of arches where Exchange & Mart used to trade. After lying empty for over a decade, the building was restored in 2001-03 as part of the Millennium Project. The factory and the house have been converted into six flats and the ground storey, with a new rendered and glazed extension, designed to accommodate a pub/restaurant. The stair tower, built for the Ragged School pupils, was demolished and replaced by a new brick and timber-clad tower containing a garage, kitchens and access to the flats. During the archaeological excavations required before the building of the extension,

New Buildings Ribbon Factory, with its new brick and timber extension that appears to have grown naturally out of the old building. There was once a steam engine here.

the well-preserved stonework of the north-west corner of the cloister range of St Mary's Priory was discovered. Most of this is preserved below the ground, but a section is visible in the lowest of the garages.

The buildings of the cycle and car industry have not fared well, although the latter only arrived in the last four years of the century. If anything, it is the office premises that have survived, although not without a struggle. The Swift office building at Parkside is now part of a hotel and was preserved after a campaign to save the building, as one of the earliest of Coventry's cycle and car industry. The two-storey, brick building is of considerably more historical than architectural interest. Britain's only entry in the 1896 London-to-Brighton 'emancipation' run, a tricar, was probably built here.

Decoration on the building is restrained, limited to horizontal stone bands and gables marking the main door, gateway and the sharp east corner of the building. Most of the interior decoration and fittings, and in particular the fine neo-Jacobean staircase in the entrance hall, were vandalized before conversion. Originally built in 1890 as a cycle factory for S. & B. Gorton, later the Quinton Cycle Company, it was taken over in 1896 by a succession of firms, under the

The Swift office building, Parkside, now a hotel. Thankfully, it was saved from demolition.

control of Harry Lawson, one of the new motor car entrepreneurs. After a short time as a chocolate factory, Swift of Coventry, who had also previously made cycles, occupied the premises to make cars from 1906. The building survived as a complete ensemble of office and production space into the late 1990s, but it was not possible to save the north-lit sheds at the rear in which all the marques were made.

Only the French *château*-style office block of the Singer works survives in Canterbury Street (1890, Harry Quick). The building was converted in the mid-1990s into Singer Hall, the communal block for Coventry University student accommodation. The building was rendered some time ago, but this has not obscured the elaborate decoration of the main entrance. Within was another impressive staircase. The production sheds were cleared for the new student blocks of flats at the rear. The firm began by making cycles in 1874 and moved on to motorcycles and cars from 1905.

A group of buildings on Far Gosford Street that began as the Calcott car factory is now better known as Astleys. The Calcott premises began as an expansion and remodelling of the earlier XL Cycle Works. The important production sheds have survived. The most obvious building, however, is the landmark office block (1896) that overlooks the lower roundabout on Sky Blue Way. The red brick and buff terracotta building is finely detailed in an eclectic mix of Renaissance styles, in vogue as the new century approached. The original doorway was on the right, but it has been blocked and the Calcott lettering above chiselled off. The main vehicular entrance is on the left-hand

Above left: The Calcott car factory office, Far Gospel Street; almost complete with its production sheds at the rear (now Astley's).

Above right: No. 38 Moor Street, Earlsdon: the office block of the Allard Cycle Company

Left: The Singer offices, Canterbury Street; now the communal block for student accommodation.

side. Between these entrances were two shallow terracotta bay windows, the left-hand one subsequently removed to provide another vehicular entrance.

Almost all of the small-scale workshops that produced cycles in the city centre have been lost. One building has survived due to its location in the less densely built-up suburb of Earlsdon, which largely escaped the Blitz and post-war redevelopment. The office block of the Allard Cycle Company fronts 38 Moor Street. It is Gothic in style with a doorway to the left and a vehicular entrance to the right. Cycles and cars were made in sheds at the rear from 1898 to 1902. The premises of the Clarendon Motor Car and Bicycle Company were situated on the same street at No. 77, but the workshop was demolished a few years ago and replaced by a surgery. The firm produced cycles in the 1890s and cars between 1902 and 1903.

The General Wolfe public house, Foleshill Road.

Pubs

Terracotta became a popular material in the late nineteenth century but was not used extensively in Coventry. It is worth mentioning the General Wolfe public house which stands prominently on Foleshill Road (*c.* 1895). It is a close and detailed study of the Tudor-Jacobean style with richly decorated triangular and Dutch gables, an octagonal corner turret and dome, two-storey bay windows and finely sculptured Classical doorways. There is another less florid pub, the Rose and Woodbine on Stoney Stanton Road (1898), in red brick and buff terracotta, with elaborate Dutch gables and a Classically-styled ground storey.

Communications

When the line from Coventry to Milverton (Leamington) was opened in 1844, the bridge that crossed the lane from Kenilworth Road to Stivichall was constructed of rough-cut sandstone with an elegant flat arch for the carriageway, flanked by two smaller arches. The two large coats of arms above the keystone of the main arch belong to the Gregory-Hood family, lords of the manor of Stivichall since the sixteenth century. The surrounding area has

Coat of Arms Bridge, Coat of Arms Bridge Road, Stivichall; a view recently spoiled by galvanized fencing.

The railway arches of Spon End, looking east, with the medieval buildings beyond.

managed to preserve a semi-rural character, which has recently been spoiled by the obtrusive fencing of the railway line and embankment by Network Rail.

The railway bridge at Spon End is of a very different scale, crossing high above the main road in a series of blue-brick arches spanning the flat valley of the Sherbourne. The arches were first built in 1850 for a branch line to Nuneaton. Twenty-three of the twenty-eight arches fell down in 1857 and the line was not reopened until 1860. They dominate the historic district of Spon End which has an interesting row of timber-framed and brick houses of various dates on the north side of the main road and was declared a Conservation Area in 2003.

TWENTIETH-CENTURY BUILDINGS

Coventry's expansion in the twentieth century was unprecedented, resulting in the erection of a huge number of buildings. This chapter will thus have to be very selective. The century does not conveniently coincide with any particular architectural style, but it will always be known for the arrival in the 1920s in Europe of the style known as International Modernism. This did not finally take solid root in England until the late 1950s and early 1960s. The twentieth century swept away a large part of the historic centre and gave Coventry a new image, not appreciated by everyone. Many of the modern buildings are humdrum, whilst some may stand the test of time and Coventry now boasts the greatest number of post-war listed buildings in any city outside London. Furthermore, local events had provided the opportunity to experiment and lead the world in the design and layout of new cities. Time alone will tell whether visitors to Coventry will as eagerly tread a path to the best of modern buildings as to the medieval guildhall of St Mary's and Holy Trinity church. A trend has at least been set, with the new cathedral voted the most popular of twentieth-century buildings.

For much of the first half of the century architecture in Coventry followed the eclecticism and profusion of styles of the Victorian period. The Edwardian period was liberated from the Gothic and developed its own distinct style, while also relying for inspiration on Tudor-Jacobean, Classical and Rennaissance-Baroque models. As elsewhere in the country, the architecture of the inter-war period could not decide which was to be the defining style. Art Deco and Moderne gained a precarious foothold in competition with a gamut of more traditional styles. Even the opportunities of post-war reconstruction in Coventry did not immediately admit the Modernist style that had been straining at the door for some time. This was architecture that claimed to be focused on pure function and the machine ethic, using new materials such as glass and reinforced concrete, unfettered by decoration. In Coventry, and England as a whole, however, the immediate post-war buildings used the 'Festival of Britain' style, where traditional materials of brick and stone cloaked the new style. The door was finally flung open in the late 1950s and early 1960s and since then Modernism has been the predominant style adopted for public, educational and commercial buildings. The Coventry entry in Pevsner's Warwickshire (1966) took up the cause enthusiastically, listing over thirty-five post-war buildings.

The style was embraced by the progressive social engineers and eminently suited to high-rise municipal blocks and rapid quick-fix construction for schools in particular. Private housing flirted with Modernism; the relationship was, however, short-lived and the neo-vernacular returned quickly in the 1980s. Modernism has to a degree been tempered, no longer as arrogant in its promise of a new age and in its condemnation of the past and disregard of context. The style continues to develop and good examples of new design have recently appeared in the city. The conservation movement, partly born out of the reaction of the worst excesses of Modernism, has an important role to play in preserving the best buildings of all ages. It is now accepted by many that the old does not have to be thrown out wholesale for the new.

Ecclesiastical

The new churches built in the burgeoning suburbs before the Second World War were for the most part traditional. Some, however, give a hint of what was to come. The ostensibly Romanesque style of St Alban's, Stoke Heath (H.B. Creswell, 1929) is Byzantine rather than Norman, hence the Mediterranean pantile roof, but there are pointed arches on the interior in the arcades and in the larger windows. All Souls' RC, Hearsall Common (1923-24, 1938 by G. Cave of Coventry) is also essentially Romanesque with a continental flavour. The stone details run out from liturgical west to east but on the north side, beyond the north transept, is a decidedly more modern tower with minimalist openings. Recent additions have unfortunately overbalanced the west front. St Barbara's in Rochester Road, Earlsdon, is unashamedly Gothic and conventional (1931-32 Austin & Paley). Two churches by N.F. Cachemaille-Day,

All Souls' church (RC), Hearsall Common; the new extension overbalances the liturgical west front.

St George's, Barkers Butts Lane, Coundon (1939) and St Luke's, Rotherham Road, Holbrooks (1939) have a considerably more modern feel, particularly on the interior. St George's is brick with distinct pointed buttresses and a slate-covered spire but on the inside there are unadorned diagonal concrete arches. St Luke's concrete roof is said to anticipate the style of the new cathedral.

St Michael's new cathedral is one of the great buildings of twentieth-century Britain and was the first post-war building to be listed. It is much loved and visited – in fact the most visited building in Coventry even forty years after its consecration. It earned the architect, Sir Basil Spence, world-renown and his knighthood. Although built between 1955 and 1962, ironically the cathedral is not regarded as the epitome of the Modernist movement. Traditionalists thought it was too modern but the Modernists criticised it for being too traditional – a cathedral in the round, such as the later Roman Catholic Cathedral in Liverpool, was felt to be more appropriate to the architecture of the age and new ways of worship. The design of the cathedral is not, however, a compromise, but without doubt a response to the site and setting. Sir Basil insisted on the retention of the old cathedral and an essential component of his scheme is the relationship between the bombed cathedral and its new successor.

The new cathedral had to be orientated from south to north with its south end facing the ruins of St Michael's. The plan is traditional, the nave is followed by the choir, which in turn gives way to the chancel. The difference between this cathedral and those preceding it is that the liturgical west end of the nave faces south and the bright light of the sun. Here was the logical and traditional place for the main entrance. Old and new cathedral also came together at this point and an architectural link could be expressed by means of a new lofty porch. Sir Basil took full advantage of the southern light and converted the 'west end' into a glass screen, etched by John Hutton with exquisite figures of angels and saints. On either side, the main walls of the cathedral are saw-toothed in order to gather more light, but in a series of tall thin windows of vivid stained glass. These can only be seen from the north and they frame the glare from the massive glazed entrance screen. The opposite end of the cathedral is dominated by the gigantic tapestry of the figure of Christ seated above the altar and designed by Graham Sutherland. Its vivid green background stands out against the white robe of Christ and the muted grey of the interior finishes. Although the nave has traditional aisles, these share the same height as the main roof, making the building more spacious inside than its dimensions would suggest. The concrete of the roof ribs is modern but an echo of the Gothic.

The outside walls are predominantly plain, smooth sandstone and appear windowless sideways on. This blankness is decidedly modern, but fortunately, the material is not. The nave walls also carry the great stained glass Baptistry window by John Piper, Jacob Epstein's statue of St Michael and Lucifer and the connection to the round Chapel of Unity. Another circular chapel, the Chapel of Industry, is attached to the side wall of the chancel via the tiny but dramatic Chapel of Gethsemane. The round chapels are reminiscent of the Gothic

St Michael's 'new' cathedral, the third in the city, with the second, old St Michael's ruins to the left.

chapter houses in cathedral monasteries such as Salisbury, York, Worcester and Lincoln. There is much else to see and admire, in particular the integration of art and architecture. What is less successful perhaps is the coat-hanger woodwork of the choir canopies, the thin electricity pylon of a fleche and the heaviness of the curved entrance canopy. These are only quibbles and the cathedral is a staggering achievement, a twentieth-century building that immediately caught the imagination of people across the world and helped symbolize the renewal of faith and the reconstruction of a city battered by war.

Sir Basil Spence's other churches in Coventry are less known. Three were built to serve the 1950s municipal estates of Willenhall (St John the Divine, Robin Hood Road, 1955-57), Tile Hill (St Oswald's, Jardine Crescent 1957-58) and Wood End (St Chad's, Hillmorton Road, 1958). They are broadly similar and in a way more 'modern' than the cathedral, the restriction on the designs imposed by the very tight budget barely concealed. All have the same group of buildings – a church, a hall, a vicarage and a free-standing open campanile – but disposed differently according to the site. The churches comprise simple, even stark, boxes constructed of a series of reinforced-concrete low-pitched arches filled with concrete panels which form the walls. There are large windows at the west ends while small windows punctuate the side concrete panels, arranged differently in each church. The four-'storey' concrete frame campaniles stand detached and have varying patterns of open infill work. These are not pretty parish complexes but their association with Basil Spence and the experimental use of a standard kit of parts, in the context of the great push to build as many municipal homes as possible, all contribute to their historical importance.

St Oswald's church, Jardine Crescent, post-war modernity or austerity?

Christchurch, Frankpledge Road, Cheylesmore. It is one of the few post-war listed churches.

Christchurch on Frankpledge Road, Cheylesmore, recently statutorily listed, was built at the same time as the Spence churches to an idiosyncratic design by A.H. Gardner (1958). It is Modernist but has not left all tradition behind. It stands on a prominence within the former Earl's Park and, as a result, its bell tower is visible from some distance away. The tower is for the most part constructed of plain brickwork with a bell storey altered a few years ago from coloured glazing to a chequerboard of two-colour brickwork. The church itself consists of three bays under flattened concrete roof arches, supported on circular concrete columns. The walls facing the street between these columns are almost entirely glazed with large stained glass panels. The description in *Coventry New Architecture* ten years after the church was built was not flattering, but, clearly, whatever qualities it has in national terms have been recognised.

Institutional

The administration of early twentieth-century Coventry had outgrown both St Mary's Hall and the Council offices, built in 1863. A large site, fronting Earl Street and St Mary Street, was cleared of a great number of interesting old houses in the 1890s. Edward Garrett and H.W. Simister designed the new Council House in Tudor style in order to be sympathetic to the immediate context. The building was begun in 1913 but its completion was delayed by the First World War. The antiquarian approach to the design lies at the opposite pole to the values of the Modern movement of half a century later. This probably reflected Coventry's view of itself as a great medieval city and not the modern city it was later to become. The red sandstone Council House has three storeys and a frontage not only to Earl Street but also to St Mary Street, linking comfortably with James Murray's Council offices (1863). The Council House also turns the corner into Hay Lane. The Earl Street frontage is symmetrical, the roof line punctuated by nine gables. The central bay over the main entrance is decorated with statues of Leofric and Godiva and of Justice in white Portland limestone and a profusion of heraldry connected with Coventry history. At the corner with St Mary Street is a square tower with a grand clock projecting diagonally out of the corner. Above the three centre gables a timber lantern marks the Council Chamber. The interior is worth seeing, particularly the Council Chamber on the first floor, evoking the spirit and grandeur of a medieval hall, and the broad, sweeping main staircase. In the long ante-room to the Council Chamber hangs one of the finest single collections of water colours of bygone Coventry by Herbert E. Cox. The corridors have round arches of the Tudor-Renaissance style with plaster decoration between groin-vaulted ceilings.

In the same year that work began on the Council House, the free Baroque style was selected for Earlsdon, Stoke and Foleshill libraries, endowed by Andrew Carnegie (1912-13). Earlsdon is a tall single-storey red-brick building with stone detailing, prominently placed at the corner of Earlsdon

The Council House – an attempt to reflect Coventry's traditional architecture and a world away from Modernism.

Earlsdon Library – one of the three Carnegie gifts to the city wrapped up in Classical style.

The Old Fire Station, awaiting a new use as the Millennium Scheme is completed around it.

Avenue North and Albany Road. The windows are high: to entice the reader Earlsdon has a prominent main door, placed asymmetrically on its long frontage, with a semi-circular broken pediment or arch. Stoke Library has its main entrance on its short frontage facing Walsgrave Road. A recent refurbishment has removed some of its original features.

In 1902 a new Fire Station was erected on Hales Street on the site of the former Jacobean-style public swimming baths. The building was designed by the City Engineer, W.E. Swindlehurst, in a free Renaissance style, using brick and stone details. It is two storey with not quite round arches on the ground floor providing the entrances for the fire engines. Originally only the four bays on the right-hand side, including the now central bay and gable, were constructed. Three houses for the stationmaster and coachmen were also built in 1902. These were demolished in 1934 and the three left-hand side bays constructed

Coventry Technical College, The Butts.

in identical style. At the rear of the building is what appears to be a bell tower which served instead to hang and dry hoses after use. The Fire Station has stood empty for many years and in the early 1990s a group of buildings at the rear, which included the stables, was demolished to make way for the new bus station. It is hoped that the recent transformation of the immediate area by the Millennium Scheme will provide opportunities for a new use.

The Classical style continued to be popular between the wars and the Technical College on The Butts was built in 1933-35 (A.W. Hoare). The detailing is stripped down to basic forms such as the cornice and the pilasters which divide each window bay. This is an imposing landmark building with two principal frontages to The Butts and Albany Road. The main entrance is marked by a projecting portico with a pediment supported on four pairs of Tuscan columns. Unfortunately, the fine entrance hall or atrium inside has been unsympathetically altered over the years.

During the inter-war period buildings were constructed in a variety of styles. The Methodist Central Hall was opened in 1932 on Warwick Lane on the site of an earlier chapel. It is essentially Tudor in style and an example of architectural conservatism for this period. A square tower and a two-storey mullioned oriel window marks the former main entrance. A few years ago the main entrance was moved to the side, which, due to post-war redevelopment, had become the most prominent frontage. The tent-like canopy here is a little incongruous. Due to the lack of a main meeting hall in Coventry, the Central Hall continues to serve as the principal venue for many events.

Comprehensive redevelopment after the war began in Broadgate. First, the ancient space was shifted westwards and then Owen Owen, now Alders, encroached on the northern side (Rolf Hellberg & Maurice Harris, 1953-35). The new west side was occupied by two mirrored buildings, Broadgate House, designed by Sir Donald Gibson and the Council's Architects' Department (1952-53) and the Hotel Leofric (W.S. Hattrell and Partners 1953-55). The co-ordination of the design was achieved as part of Sir

Right: The Methodist Central Hall, Warwick Lane.

Below: Broadgate House – one of the first buildings of the post-war master plan on the left flank of the Upper Precinct. The bridge to Hertford Street was on the extreme left.

The Leofric, slightly different in detail to Broadgate House, on the opposite flank of the Upper Precinct, with Alders, formerly Owen Owen, to the right.

Donald's plan to provide a unified setting on the west side of Broadgate and a gateway to the intended Upper Precinct. Broadgate House was also slung across Hertford Street, allowing traffic to pass below, and terminated at its east end with a clock tower. The old line of Hertford Street was filled in between the clock tower and the pre-war bank. The area below the bridge was inelegantly blocked in about 1970-71, after Hertford Street was closed to traffic in 1969 and subsequently pedestrianized. This group of buildings is of historical and urban design significance, as they set in motion the comprehensive redevelopment of the city centre and determined its style. Their architectural merit is less obvious and they were criticized at the time and for many years later for their timidity – in other words, their lack of courage in grasping Modernism, the extensive use of brick and stone obscuring the functionalism of reinforced concrete frames. Certainly visitors do not flock to this area to appreciate the architecture; any excitement is limited to the suspense just before the hour is struck, waiting for Lady Godiva to emerge on her rickety horse from behind the doors in the clock tower. The traditional materials have, however, mellowed and do not offend. The same cannot be said about the Cathedral Lanes Shopping Centre and its canopy that eventually muscled into the east side of Broadgate in 1989-90.

The Herbert Art Gallery and Museum (1954–59) used the same combination of brick and stone, as west Broadgate (Herbert, Son & Sawday of Leicester). Work had started on a Neo-Classical building just before Second World War, but the design was seen as too old-fashioned by the post-war modernists and was eventually abandoned. In 1969, however, the 'modern' building was regarded as being 'dreadfully dated', particularly for its use of sculpture and decoration. It would be interesting to know what the late 1960s opinion would have been of the re-erection a few years ago of the two Walter Ritchie reliefs against one of the vast expanses of brick facing Jordan Well. These had originally been fixed as two separate panels above a water feature, now demolished, in the Upper Precinct. Parts of the building are being altered significantly, inside and out, in 2003-04, and so time has already run out for appreciating many of its qualities.

Arthur Ling, successor to Sir Donald Gibson, was responsible for the design of the Belgrade Theatre, which may explain the more obvious use of concrete and its simpler expression of form (1955-58). It was the first repertory theatre built in the country after the Second World War. Brick is used on the Corporation Street frontage, but the building is supported on round concrete columns before the colonnade of shops on the ground floor.

The Herbert Art Gallery and Museum with the Walter Ritchie reliefs, originally situated on the Upper Precinct, on the right.

The Belgrade Theatre, now statutorily listed.

The frontage to Upper Well Street is concrete and glass and defines the front of house. The concrete panels flanking the main area of glazing correspond to the two staircases, which provide access to the circle. The main entrance to the theatre is skewed to the left with a theatre bar facing out into Corporation Street. Major extensions towards Bond Street, including a new theatre, are planned but there will be no radical alteration to the main *foyer* area or to the external elevations described here.

Purer Modernist architecture in Coventry is found at the early 1950s Woodlands Comprehensive School, consisting of thirteen individual blocks erected on a greenfield site on the western edge of the expanding city (Broad Lane, Tile Hill). The campus of buildings formed one of the earliest purpose-built comprehensive schools in the country. The school was designed by the City Architect's Department under Sir Donald Gibson, in collaboration with the Ministry of Education's Development Group under Stirrat Johnson Marshall (1953-55). In order to build quickly and cheaply, standard structural members were used. The gaps between the steel frames were filled with flat, lightweight panels and no attempt was made to dress the structure up. Around the corner aluminium parts made by Bristol Aeroplane Company were used for Limbrick Wood Junior and Infant School (1951-52). Both these schools are now statutorily listed, not without causing some local controversy. The unique construction of Limbrick Wood School will make the maintenance and sympathetic alteration of the buildings very difficult.

Another Modernist building designed just before the end of the 1950s and only recently listed is Coventry Station, the first post-war railway station constructed by British Rail. It was finished in 1962 to a design by W.R. Headley, the then architect for British Rail, Midlands Region. A single great concrete slab covers the whole building, providing both a canopy for those arriving at the station from the city centre and the roof for the concourse and the stairs that connect the four platforms. Large plate-glass widows define the concourse on two sides; this light, lofty and airy space is the most successful part of the building. Unfortunately, the station is closely surrounded

Woodlands School, Broad Lane, Tile Hill, a statutorily listed comprehensive school.

Coventry Railway Station, another statutorily listed post-war building.

by more banal 1960s buildings and there is no obvious visual link with the city centre. There are plans currently being developed to rectify this matter, based on a direct and generous boulevard to Greyfriars Green.

Another first for the post-war city were the swimming baths in Fairfax Street (1962-66). They were designed in the mid-1950s by the City Architects' Department, led by J.M. McLellan. Built to contemporary Olympic standards, the swimming pool was received with great approbation and was considered a feather in the cap for the city authorities. It is certainly an impressive building, with its great flat gull-wing roof soaring over the huge space of the main pool. The best frontage has a huge glazed screen but is no longer appreciated by many, having been hemmed in by buildings around a minor pedestrian route. In facing south it suffers the inevitable glare of the sun. The main public entrance is on Fairfax Street, the dark north side. Strictly speaking it is the back of the building, which explains the great mass of plain brickwork, though it has its own grandeur. How quickly a building becomes obsolete! The swimming pool is no longer considered to meet modern standards and the City Council and sports authorities wish to demolish and begin again. There is one problem, however, for in recognition of its architectural and historical interest it was statutorily listed in 1997.

It is great leap from the 1960s to the end of the century when, after the economic decline of the late 1970s to the late 1980s, good public buildings are again being erected in the city. Two new buildings of the revival of the past few years are worthy of comment. The new library for Coventry University is spectacular and like no other building in Coventry. Designed by Short &

Left: Coventry Swimming Baths, from the north east.

Opposite: The library; at last Coventry University possesses a great building.

Associates, it was constructed between 1998 and 2000 and based on principles of energy conservation and eco-friendliness. The library is essentially based on four square floors but this regular shape is not obvious in the elevations. Ten ventilation towers, reminiscent of the medieval towers of Siena in Italy, are positioned round the periphery of the building. The towers act as flues drawing air through the building, gathering and distributing ambient heat from people and computers and expelling stale air at the top. The building is clad in a honey-coloured brick and the complex geometry of the towers and other architectural elements presents a visually stunning composition that changes according to the viewpoint. One of the best views is from Whitefriars monastery.

Despite the name, the vast majority of Warwick University lies within Coventry. It was established in the late 1960s on the rural fringes on the south-west side of the city. The early buildings form part of one of the grandest Modernist conceptions in England by Yorke, Rosenberg, Mardall in purest style. It was not to be completed. The campus has mellowed over the years as the university gradually strengthened its reputation, but it remains a strong enclave of modern design tempered by the more domestic-scaled, brick residential complexes, which continue to spread across open countryside.

A very different building graces the Millennium Project's Cloister Garden. Designed by MacCormac, Jamieson and Pritchard of London, who were master planers and architects for the whole scheme, it was constructed in

113

2000-01 (page 26.). A modern building in an ancient setting, it sits comfortably within both the historic environment and the new gardens designed by Dominic Scott of Robert Rummey Associates of Sevenoaks, Kent. The lowest section of the south wall is formed by the thick sandstone north wall of St Mary's Cathedral, the middle section of a seventeenth-century sandstone wall and new courses of Hollington sandstone on the top. Lastly, there is a narrow clerestory. The building demonstrates how effective a north-facing glass screen can be, with a view onto the walled enclosure of the Cloister Garden. The side walls are all smooth Hollington sandstone, as on the new cathedral, and the roof is an aircraft-like wing. The building houses the best of the finds from the 1999-2002 archaeological excavations. A hole has been deliberately left open within the floor of the building to show the level of the medieval cloister and the position of a doorway into the former cathedral. MacCormac, Jamieson and Pritchard also designed the adjacent Cathedral Office and the buildings that surround Priory Place. Their first commission in Coventry, however, was for the highly acclaimed Cable and Wireless College at Westwood Heath Road (1992). This is a striking and innovative reinterpretation of the residential college with dramatic, tiled, curving roofs of the single-storey teaching blocks, linked by a central facility and an oval court to the strongly modelled, three-storey residential blocks. The landscaping is fully integrated with the architecture to create a series of enclosed spaces and

The Cable and Wireless College, Westwood Heath Road. This 'ocular' space is elegantly enclosed to form the hub of the complex.

vistas, one of which terminates with the sports and social club and its sunken 'Roman' bath. Without doubt this is a listed building of the future.

Houses

Coventry is better known for its experiments in producing housing as quickly as possible after the losses of the Second World War than for architect-designed individual houses for the middle classes. There are some worthy houses in the late Victorian-Edwardian domestic style in the Davenport Road and Warwick Road area. Earlsdon has a variety of generous houses built before and after the First World War using a similar vernacular style. Further south along Kenilworth Road many of the large houses hidden among the trees of the Spinney are disappointing, their architecture not matching the grandeur of one of the most spectacular entries into a city anywhere in the country. This broad and green ride is enhanced by the local topography of Gibbet Hill, from which there is a most impressive vista north towards the city centre, but only of trees. This area deserves some great houses.

There is an interesting contrast between the homes built for the elderly in Lady Herbert's Garden (1935, 1937) and the 1950s bungalows in Wellington Gardens, Spon End. Lady Herbert's Homes are arranged in a double row facing each other and finish at the town wall. They are one of the few genuine 'Arts and Crafts' buildings in Coventry, though they were conceived when the movement was more or less spent. Lady Herbert's Garden, laid out along the line of the town wall, had deteriorated in recent years, but was restored in 2001 as part of the Millennium Scheme. Its historical value was recognised by its recent addition to the National Register of Parks and Gardens and the listing of the almshouses, the boundary wall and garden shelter. The Wellington Gardens bungalows, also intended for the elderly, are simple in form, but arranged around a green, providing a pleasant environment in this inner-city suburb. An interesting relief decorates a community centre. The bungalows are now included in Spon End Conservation Area.

In the post-war period a number of private houses were built in Modernist style. Particularly worthy of note are houses in the Kenilworth Road area by the Warwickshire architect Robert Harvey, whose style was heavily influenced by Frank Lloyd Wright: 'South Winds' in Cryfield Grange Road, 9 Gibbet Hill Road, 112 and 114 Kenilworth Road. A small estate of interesting houses with steep mono-pitched roofs and open-plan

The Lady Herbert's almshouses.

interiors was laid out in the early 1960s in Walsgrave (Nordic Drift and Oslo Gardens). These attempted to escape the vernacular tradition, but the Nordic style never caught on. Most of these houses have been 'improved,' frequently compromising the original design.

Municipal housing was not timid in its embrace of Modernism and this has been blamed, not always justifiably, for its lack of popularity and attendant social ills. Criticism has been concentrated on the high-rise blocks. The most distinct and numerous of these are the Hillfields slabs with their multi-coloured panels and gull-wing roofs, which rise in echelon up the hill to the area once known as Prior's Harnall in the medieval period. Marching across the elevated north side of the city centre are three blocks of flats, which were constructed in the mid-1960s using the lift-slab system. The floors were jacked up one by one to their final position around a central concrete core. Their design is not subtle, the windows peering out from deep recesses behind the solid bands of concrete forming the balconies. Alpha House in Barras Heath was the earliest tower block in the world to use another variation – the jack-block system (1962-63). Here there are no balconies but simple flat elevations of glazing and panels.

Pubs

A great many early twentieth century pubs were demolished in the Blitz and in post-war redevelopment. Three good examples of inter-war pubs survive deep in their contemporary suburbs. The Toll Gate, Birmingham Road, is the most 'Moderne' in style, with the emphasis on the horizontal, with walls rendered, corners rounded, the roof flat and the broad metal-framed windows. The Pilot, Catesby Road, Radford, has recently been listed as a good example of a 1930s pub with a relatively unspoilt 'Moderne' interior. In contrast to The Toll Gate, however, it is brick-faced with a

The streamlined form of one of Coventry's first Moderne public houses, The Toll Gate, Birmingham Road.

The Pilot, Catesby Road, relatively conventional on the outside but with many of the original fittings inside.

Brown's, Earl Street, a success from the start with an even more dramatic interior.

steeply pitched roof. The tall metal windows provide a vertical emphasis. The traditional form is emphasized by the half octagon flanking wings with pyramidal roofs. The Cedars on Barkers Butts Lane has a Mediterranean look, emphasized by its pantile roof. It has a lively frontage with set-back Dutch gables, flat metal windows, a canopied sun trap window and rendered walls. The city's only interesting post-war pub, until Brown's, was the modernist The Rose (Yorke, Harper and Harvey, 1964). Apparently, in the Frank Lloyd Wright tradition, its plan is a stylized rose.

In 1998 the site of the unfinished pre-war museum was taken over by a new pub/restaurant (architects, Baynes & Co., Cawston near Rugby). Brown's moved from the Lower Precinct to a building that was courageous both in architectural and commercial terms. It is difficult to define the style: the exterior has rough-cut sandstone walls, large expanses of glazing and a great curving copper roof that almost hits the ground at the rear. Internally, it has a 'retro' 1950s feel with plenty of exposed timber. The ground floor is relatively dark but reaches upward to the curving ribs of the roof, whilst the upper floor, which wraps round this space, is light and airy. This is one of Coventry's most successful 1990s buildings.

Industrial
Most of the interesting industrial buildings of the twentieth century appear to have been built in the first fifty years. The arrival of the 'crinkly tin shed'

118

in the post-war period has unfortunately produced dull industrial buildings that are repeated *ad infinitum* across the whole country.

Many of the historic, but often unspectacular, factories of the early car and cycle industries have been demolished. The finest was the Rudge (later GEC) motorcycle works in Spon Street, that was removed from the skyline in 1991. The buildings of the cycle industry are now few and far between. An example of a building with some architectural pretensions is the office of Challenge Cycle Works, constructed in 1906 on Foleshill Road, opposite George Eliot Road. It is classical in form and detail, symmetrical with shallow projecting bays at each end and a projecting central entrance, all emphasized with bands of stone and brick. A high parapet between piers decorated with the firm's insignia gives prominence to the end bays.

In 1896 the Coventry-based Daimler Motor Company produced the first four-wheeled motor cars in the country. The firm had occupied on beneficial terms a former cotton spinning mill on the Coventry Canal, a site apparently chosen by chance. Only two buildings remain from the vast complex. The Power House (1907) was not intended for a steam engine or steam turbine, but for new-fangled electricity generators. It is a large brick building, sadly the worse for wear, with cast-iron round-headed windows,

The former Challenge cycle works, Foleshill Road.

some blocked, and a roof vent to cool the generators. Its vast size is best appreciated from inside; all the generating plant was stripped out long ago but part of the overhead crane survives. Not far away, at the main entrance to the site on Sandy Lane, is the four-storey Daimler office block (1907-08). This is a plain building, even severe, with decoration limited to horizontal stone bands at the level of the window cills and lintels.

It is a little-known fact that the William Morris building in Gosford Street, refurbished by Coventry University in 1994, is in fact two separate buildings with different origins. The west (upper) part of the originally four-storey building was built during the First World War, in early 1916, by the displaced French firm Hotchkiss to manufacture machine guns. In 1923 Morris took over the premises and built a multi-storey block in similar style on the lower side as an engine works. Many Coventrians remember the great fire that destroyed much of the rear and upper parts of the building in 1964 when it was in use as a government store. The new upper floors added by the university contrast with the simple lines of the earlier industrial architecture dominated by large 'shop' windows, but the result has been a success.

The Courtaulds buildings have dominated Foleshill Road for a century. The company established a factory for the production of rayon in 1904 and the first fibre was made at the end of 1905. Courtaulds could also claim to have spun the first nylon yarn in the country in 1941. By this time a

The William Morris Building, University of Coventry, Gosford Street. The upper half was a machine-gun works, the lower half a car engine works.

Former Courtaulds,
Foleshill Road (Tower
Court) with a new glazed
side elevation.

large complex of multi-storey buildings had developed on both sides of
Foleshill Road. The three street frontage buildings (1905-10), dominated by
a clock tower, form an impressive group using a deep red and rich brick with
Classical details in terracotta. The complex has lost its original production
sheds, which originally lay on the south side and along the canal. The
frontage buildings were under threat of demolition about a decade ago, but
they were fortunately saved and converted into an office and technology
'park' by the City Council in the mid-1990s.

Despite the growth of the city in the inter-war period, there is a distinct lack
of good examples of Art-Deco architecture in Coventry. The best example, but
on a modest scale, is the MGA building on Birmingham Road, Allesley, on the
very edge of the city. Its most impressive feature is the centrally placed
entrance hall and staircase, which displays a glory of curves, glass blocks and
wood panelling. The lumpish Coventry Theatre in Hales Street in the city
centre (1937), a variety theatre, lately a bingo hall, was demolished amid some
controversy in 2002 as part of the Millennium Scheme. The historically
significant 'shadow' factory on the western fringe of the city (Banner Lane)
was commissioned by the government in 1939-40 as part of the rearmament
programme. This factory was run by the Standard Company on a day-to-day
basis for the production of Hercules engines. The buildings have been owned
by Massey Ferguson for some time, but the future of the firm and its extensive

premises is uncertain. The present Jaguar factory in a similar semi-rural environment to the north of Allesley village has its origins in the Daimler No. 2 shadow factory.

Commercial

By the inter-war period substantial commercial buildings in a variety of styles were appearing in the city centre. The Classical portico of the National Westminster Bank (National Provincial 1930, architect F.C.R. Palmer) dominated the south end of Broadgate for a few years until the buildings it overlooked were obliterated in the Blitz. The Cathedral Lanes shopping centre now obscures the earlier vista. In contrast to the red brick and stone columns and pediment of the Nat West Bank, the adjacent Lloyds Bank at 30 High Street (1932, Buckland & Haywood) offers a frontage based on a great triumphal arch in Portland limestone almost devoid of any windows. The side elevations of these two banks, as they run down the first part of Greyfriars Lane, transformed the character and scale of this ancient lane to Warwick.

By contrast, mock timber framing was employed later in the 1930s at the other end of Broadgate on the site of the demolished buildings of Great Butcher Row (1937). The steel-frame building, originally and appropriately named 'Priory Gate', is clad in a rich Tudoresque profusion of applied

The National Westminster Bank, Broadgate.

timber-frame, jetties, bay windows, balconies, gables and tall brick chimneys. The composition certainly harmonizes with the genuinely medieval Lych Gate Cottages to which it was attached. The present 'Flying Standard' name has no link with the site, for here once stood the gate that led into the forecourt of the cathedral of St Mary. By further contrast, the west side of the new Trinity Street (1937) attempted to be as modern as it could be with flat, undecorated brick façades, steel windows and flat roofs.

Right: Lloyds Bank, on High Street.

Below: Wetherspoons, Trinity Street, with the Lych Gate Cottages to the right. It was originally called 'Priory Gate', a historically accurate name.

Neither Classical nor Tudor vernacular were to outlast the war and the Sir Donald Gibson version of the Modern Movement was transferred from Broadgate to the Upper Precinct in the early 1950s. This was the style of the first part of the earliest large-scale pedestrianized shopping precinct in the country (1951-54). An essential part of the Gibson plan was to reorientate the ancient Smithford Street onto a new line to create a vista eastwards towards the medieval spire of St Michael's Cathedral. This has, to a considerable extent, been spoilt by the escalator and ramp in the Upper Precinct and the canopy and roof of Cathedral Lanes in the middle distance. Fortunately, the spire is the second highest in the country. Another important element of the scheme was the two-tier shopping provision, but this was never successful.

The original Upper Precinct scheme underwent considerable change in the 1990s followed by the Lower Precinct (1957-60, City Architect's Department under Arthur Ling) at the turn of the new millennium. The Lower Precinct rejected the brown-brick cladding of the Upper Precinct in favour of a dark green stone (*Serpentino* marble) and perforated anodized aluminium panels, but could not resist squat gables. The Round Café, a witty piece of Modernism planted in the centre like a mushroom, helped enliven the surrounding architecture. It was restored in 2003. The two shopping levels work better here

The Upper Precinct, looking east towards the focal point of the spire of the old cathedral of St Michael's.

The Lower Precinct, reopened in 2002 under a new glass roof. The round café was saved and is now trading again.

as the approach from the Precinct crossing coincides with the upper tier. Now a vast glass roof, supported on massive tree-like steel supports, provides complete cover. The widening of the ramp down to the lower level necessitated the removal of the surviving Gordon Cullen tile mural depicting the history of Coventry. These tiles have been reset and are seen, strangely enough, to better advantage at the tunnel-like west exit. A bay of shops on the south side were removed to provide a new route (Sherbourne Arcade) to the remarkable circular layout of the Retail Market (1957), sadly located in a service area at the rear of the shopping precinct. Pedestrianization was introduced to Smithford Way and Market Way (1951-54), originally intended to be used by vehicles, and then extended to Shelton Square (1960), the City Arcade (1960-62) and Bull Yard (1965-68). Hertford Street was also pedestrianized in 1970 with some of the original street retained in a rather bizarre but successful mixture. The remaining three vistas from the Precinct crossing were eventually obscured by tower blocks built in the late 1960s and early 1970s.

Miscellany

Pevsner describes Lady Godiva's statue, sculpted in bronze by Sir William Reid-Dick (commissioned 1937, unveiled 1949) as 'corny', but this is a view that is not shared by Coventrians, who have become attached to this mythological image of Coventry. Conventional perhaps, but the demure Lady Godiva has had the misfortune to be placed beneath the canvas canopy of Cathedral Lanes, where the diffuse light drains all life from her.

In 2001 five timber sheds/summer houses in Stoney Road allotments, Cheylesmore, were, to everyone's surprise, listed. They display a more-than-average degree of sturdiness and architectural decoration for allotment buildings, in the form of decorated barge boards and mock timber-framing. They symbolize a bygone age when the allotment played a more important role in the economy and recreation of local people.

Telephone kiosks may not be regarded as buildings, but two in Warwick Road have been statutorily listed. They are of the K-6 type, which was designed by Sir Giles Gilbert Scott and introduced in 1936. They constitute a much-loved piece of street furniture, seen as representing Britain at home and abroad. This type and its sturdy successors are getting rarer by the month, as the wretchedly intrusive mobile phone leaves them unused and obsolete.

Who knows what new buildings will appear in this ancient city in the next few decades. Some are being designed at this very moment, but the last few years have proved yet again that well designed buildings breed pride, optimism and economic well being. Let us hope that any successor to this book in the distant future will carry with confidence plenty of examples from the twenty-first century.

A fast-disappearing item of street furniture, the K-6 telephone box.

FURTHER READING

Alcock, N.W., *People at Home Living in a Warwickshire Village, 1580-1800*, (1993)

Basset, S., *Anglo-Saxon Coventry and its Churches*, Dugdale Society Occasional Papers, No. 41 (2001)

Charles, F.W.B., *Conservation of Timber Buildings* (1984)

Coss, P.R., *The Early Records of Medieval Coventry* (1986)

Conservation Team, Coventry City Council, *Coventry City Centre Trail* (1993)

Conservation Team, Coventry City Council, *Coventry Car Factories* (1996)

Colvin, H., *A Biographical Dictionary of British Architects, 1600-1840*, 3rd edition (1995)

Davis, R.H.C., *The Early History of Coventry*, Dugdale Society Occasional Papers No. 2 (1976)

Demidowicz, G., *Coventry's First Cathedral The Cathedral and Priory of St Mary* (1994)

Demidowicz, G., *A History of Blue Coat School and the Lych Gate Cottages* (2000)

Lewison, G., Billingham, R., *Coventry New Architecture* (1969)

Pevsner, N., Wedgewood, A., *The Buildings of England, Warwickshire* (1966)

Prest, J., *The Industrial Revolution in Coventry* (1960)

Conservation Team, Coventry City Council, *Spon Street Townscape Scheme* (1993)

Richardson, K., *Twentieth Century Coventry* (1972)

Victoria County History of Warwick, Vol VIII Coventry and Warwick (1969)

Walter, P., *History in our Hands* (1989)

City Council Heritage Open Day leaflets published on many buildings

Researching Buildings

A principal source for nearly a thousand nationally and locally listed buildings in the city are the records held by the Conservation Team in the City Development Directorate. The amount of information contained on each building can, however, vary greatly in size and content. Other important repositories are the City Record Office, Mandela House and Local Studies in the Central Library, where there are many original plans and illustrations. The huge collection of property deeds and rentals at the Record Office are also helpful in any study of lost Coventry buildings. Further afield, information can be found at Warwick Record Office and in the Public Record Office at Kew, London. There is much useful work still to be done on the architecture and history of Coventry buildings.

George Demidowicz
24 June 2003